The Which? Guide to
Shopping
on the Internet

The Which? Guide to
Shopping
on the Internet

Compiled by SIAN MORRISSEY

CONSUMERS' ASSOCIATION

Which? Books are commissioned and researched by
Consumers' Association and published by
Which? Ltd, 2 Marylebone Road, London NW1 4DF
Email address: books@which.net

Distributed by The Penguin Group:
Penguin Books Ltd, 27 Wrights Lane, London W8 5TZ

Copyright © 2001 Which? Ltd
First edition April 2001
With thanks to: Claire Gordon-Brown, David Kenning, Jonquil Lowe,
Roger Moore

British Library Cataloguing in Publication Data
A catalogue record for this book is available from the British Library

ISBN 0 85202 857 1

For a full list of Which? books, please write to:
Which? Books, Castlemead, Gascoyne Way, Hertford X, SG14 1LH
or access our web site at: www.which.net

Cover: Price Watkins Design
Illustrations: Toby Morison

Typeset by Saxon Graphics Ltd, Derby
Printed and bound in Great Britain by Clays Ltd, St Ives plc

This is the first-ever publication
to contain a list of Which? Web Traders

For more details, see Part 3

Contents

Part 3

A guide to Which? Web Traders

The Which? Web Trader scheme

Which? Web Traders

Part 4

Information sites

Appendix: Setting yourself up with the Internet

Index

Web site report form

Introduction

Who would have thought, just a few short years ago, that
going shopping could ever have meant just sitting down in
front of a computer? Or that we would want to shop in this
way? Probably not too many people – but according to a
survey carried out by Which? Online and MORI in May
2000, nearly half of all Internet users in the UK (nearly six
million people) have shopped online and a quarter of surfers
now regularly use the Net to shop, and the numbers are
growing all the time.

New sites are going online daily. UK Internet users are
already among the keenest online shoppers in the world. For
example, a survey published in 2001 by Datamonitor on
shopping for groceries showed that British consumers are
more likely than any other nation, including the USA, to buy
groceries online.

As unmetered Internet access becomes the norm and
worries about the cost of the time spent online diminish,
browsing the online shops could well become a major leisure
activity. But the huge number and range of shopping sites
can seem daunting even to an experienced Internet user. It
can be hard to know where to start and when you have
wasted time trying to get an order through for the
umpteenth time on a poorly designed, temperamental site, it
can be tempting to give up altogether.

This book aims to dispel some of the myths that surround
shopping on the Internet. It guides you through the maze of
online shopping sites, shows you how to find what you want
and boosts your confidence. It also points out the pitfalls and
tells you what to do if something goes wrong.

The extensive Web Directory in Part 2 provides a guide to
and reviews of a wide range of sites catering for all sorts of
shopping needs. Whether you want to buy a kitchen table,
treat yourself to some designer clothes, purchase a power

tool, set up a new savings scheme or order your groceries, the Web Directory can point you in the right direction. Many of the sites listed are Which? Web Traders – members of the scheme set up by Consumers' Association to ensure that consumers get a fair deal online.

Part 3 comprises the first-ever listing of Which? Web Traders to appear in print. Use it to help you shop with confidence from around 900 sites.

You may worry about giving your credit card number online and the risk of fraud. You might also be concerned about your goods not being delivered or not being what you expected – after all, you have not been able to examine them as you would have been able to do in a shop. This guide addresses such concerns and offers suggestions on how to reduce the risks. It also tells you how to purchase goods from abroad with minimal hassle and explores the highs and lows of buying and selling at Internet auction sites.

The book assumes that you already have a basic knowledge of the Internet but the section 'Getting Started on the Internet' should help you out if you are starting from scratch.

The Internet is constantly evolving, so to predict exactly how our shopping habits will be affected by it in the long run is difficult. What seems certain, however, is that shopping on the Internet is not going to replace traditional trips to 'bricks-and-mortar' shops and transform the high street. Much more likely is that the two types of shopping will co-exist, with consumers using both forms of shopping depending on what they want, the time they have available and their general lifestyle. Whether you are simply after the occasional cut-price CD or have plans to shop on the Internet for everything from your groceries to your furniture and holidays, *The Which? Guide to Shopping on the Internet* will enable you to make the most of the online shopping revolution.

Part 1

The why, how and where of shopping on the Internet

Why shop online?

1

There are many good reasons to try shopping online. The choice of retail sites is huge and you can find a real bargain if you know where to look. You can also find unusual (sometimes even unique) items that are unlikely to be in the high-street stores. Recent changes to the way you are charged for using the Internet mean that worrying about the cost of the time you spend online will increasingly become a thing of the past. New Europe-wide laws covering shopping on the Internet now give consumers more protection than before.

How shopping online started

The Internet was until relatively recently a shopping-free zone. At the beginning of the 1990s, it was used mainly by universities and research organisations, government bodies and non-profit groups as a forum for sharing research and science-related information. It was only in 1994 that the Internet opened up to commercial interests. Pizza Hut was one of the first companies to see the potential of the Net, setting up an experimental online pizza delivery service in California. At that time there were not enough potential customers linked to the Net for the service to work and it folded within months. That year, however, computer equipment and software was beginning to be sold commercially online, and a number of US banks began to offer online services.

From then on, there was no looking back. As more and more people connected to the Internet, so the number of retail sites in the USA grew. Within a few years some UK sites were up and running.

Shopping via the Internet is now becoming a key part of retail economy. The predictions are that by 2005, close to ten per cent of retail sales in the UK will be through online shopping, with around £20 billion being spent by consumers at retail sites. This is a massive leap from the 0.25 per cent of online sales in 1999.

Starting to shop

Thousands of retailers now trade on the Internet. Tracking down the ones that interest you may initially seem a daunting task. This book will help you shop online confidently and effectively. It tells you how to find the best shopping sites for what you want and what to do once you get to them.

If you are new to the Internet you may prefer to find your feet with the medium first rather than leaping in and shopping straight away. According to a Which? Online/MORI poll in May 2000, around 23 per cent of all Internet users now regularly shop online, compared to ten per cent in 1999. One in four users have now bought books; the other most popular products being CDs, videos, flights, holidays and computer software and hardware.

Confidence with using the Internet is clearly a key influence on when people start to use it to shop regularly. Concerns such as worries about online credit-card fraud, the cost of using the Internet or even a frustrating first experience trying to shop online can put people off. Recent changes to the way consumers are charged for Internet access should help. Oftel, the regulator for the telecoms industry, introduced measures in 2001 which should allow millions of people to have unlimited access to the Internet without worrying about running up high call charges.

What you can buy

Books, CDs, videos and DVDs, computers and software are the most popular products purchased online, but you can shop on the Internet for everything from face creams to fridges. With figures indicating that around one-third of the UK population is now linked up to the Internet, it's not surprising that many thousands of retailers have their own web sites nowadays – or are at least planning one. Despite the much-publicised difficulties faced by some Internet-only retailers and reports at the end of 2000 that commercial web sites were closing down at the rate of one a day, the UK's online shopping market is gradually becoming part-and-parcel of the retail operation.

You can shop at sites that are part of well-known high-street chains and department stores or at those set up by the smallest specialist stores. You can go to sites that are run by retailers who only sell on the Internet and to shopping sites that do not actually sell anything them-selves but that link you to a range of retailers' sites.

As well as physical products, you can buy tickets for shows and concerts or for aeroplane, train or coach journeys. You can sort out your insurance, mortgage, shares and even your pension online. Buying on the Internet has become part of everyday life with myriad different products available that you would expect to be able to buy as a matter of course on the telephone or by visiting shops. In addition, it can be a much more convenient and often cheaper method of shopping than buying via more traditional routes.

Six reasons to start shopping online

- It can be less stressful. Traditional shopping can be an enjoyable experience but it often isn't. Anyone who has spent a hectic Saturday, possibly with children in tow, battling through the traffic to a packed shopping centre only to find that the item you want is out of stock, can appreciate the convenience of shopping from your own home, at the click of a mouse.

- It can be cheaper. Competition between online retailers is fierce and this can have a beneficial effect on prices. Retailers that sell only online do not have the overheads of 'bricks and mortar' shops and can pass these savings on to consumers. Even retailers that sell by traditional means as well as via the Internet, sometimes offer the same goods cheaper if you buy them online. Remember, however, that 'online' does not always mean cheaper. It can still be worth ringing or visiting high-street stores and comparing their prices with those on a selection of web sites.

- The Internet is a massive shop window for a huge range of products to which you might not have had access, or even knew existed, before you started using it. You can now browse, at any time you choose, that top West End store you normally visit only once or twice a year.

- The Net can save you time, especially when you know what you want. Buying CDs, a washing machine, some new clothes for the children or your weekly groceries can be done in minutes rather than hours. Shop when it suits you rather than during traditional shop opening hours.

- You are more in control. You do not have to endure pushy sales assistants or high-pressure selling. True, you will often be faced with a barrage of advertising when you visit many sites. If you don't like what you see, you can simply click to another site.
- It can be fun! Once you get into the habit of browsing Internet shops, it can be hard to stop. Beware of impulse buying, though – you may have to learn to keep that credit card at a safe distance from your computer.

The downside of Internet shopping

Prospective Internet shoppers have high expectations of their online shopping experiences. They want to be able to find what they want quickly, order with minimum hassle and receive the goods within days. These are not unrealistic expectations but the reality of shopping online does not always live up to the expectations or the hype.

Six reasons for not shopping online

- You may worry about your credit card details being misused. This is a common concern and the occasional newspaper story about Internet scams fans the flames of doubt. But using your credit card over the Internet carries no more risk than using it for any other shopping transaction (for more on this see pages 39–40).
- Slow sites. Some web sites can take what can seem like an age to load and if you want to look at more complicated images like video clips, the wait can sometimes be highly frustrating.

- Difficulties in placing your order or finding what you want on the site. This is often due to poor site design or maintenance. In a recent *Which?* report (November 2000) on ordering goods over the Internet, researchers ordering products from 12 sites selling books, CDs, computer hardware and software, and food, experienced many problems such as not being able to locate the item they wanted, technical hitches, or difficulties carrying an order through to completion.

- Site is too personally intrusive. Sometimes you need to give what can seem like a lot of personal information to sites when you register with them or order. Sites also often place a small information file on your computer known as a 'cookie'. These collect information on what you look at or order when you visit a site. Even though any information you provide to a site should not be passed on to a third party without your permission, not all sites may respect your wishes. According to research undertaken by Consumers International, over two-thirds of web sites surveyed collected some type of personal data during a visit to a site; just over a half of the sites that collected information had a privacy policy, but only one-third highlighted any privacy policy when collecting information.

- Delivery difficulties. Sites sometimes promise more than they can deliver in terms of timing. Always check the delivery charges (if any), the method of delivery (courier or post) and time scale on the site. If you are still not sure, confirm by phone with the company. For more on delivery, see Chapter 4.

- Problems with goods from certain types of sites. Some sites deal in products that can be problematic. Dealers selling counterfeit goods, for example, can be attracted to auction sites because it is easier for them to stay relatively anonymous. Generally speaking, buying from an auction site means you have less legal protection if something goes wrong than if you buy from an ordinary retailer's site. (For more on buying and selling at online auctions, see Chapter 6.) Sites that sell prescription drugs have also faced criticism. Research carried out for *Health Which?* in 2000 found sites willing to supply researchers with drugs such as Viagra when for medical reasons they should not have done.

Try before you buy

Online shopping certainly is not perfect. A recent international survey by the management consultants AT Kearney found that as many as 75 per cent of UK shoppers trying to buy goods on the Internet abandon their attempts. Prospective shoppers often complained that too much on-screen information needed to be provided, and as many as 40 per cent said they could not find the product they wanted. However, technical aspects of site design and customer service standards are improving. Sites that do not improve and move with consumers' expectations will lose customers.

It's important to bear in mind that millions of people worldwide successfully shop online all the time. Many sites are attractive, very easy to use and deliver on time. So do not let one or two disappointing experiences stop you from experimenting. The only way to find out whether you will become a committed regular online shopper is to try out a few sites until you find a selection you are happy with.

The basics of shopping online

You have to have a few key items before you start your online shopping experience. You will need to have set up your access to the Internet by registering with a company that provides you with a route to the Net – these companies are known as Internet Service Providers or ISPs. Unless you are likely to become a very heavy Internet user, in which case you may want to opt for a high-speed digital phone connection, you will need a modem too. This is the piece of equipment that dials the telephone number of the ISP and connects your computer with the ISP's much more powerful computer (called a server). Once this connection is made you are linked to the Internet.

Some modems are built into computers, others are in the form of a separate box. It is worth getting the fastest modem you can afford if you want to be able to browse the Internet with relative ease. (For more detailed information, see Appendix.)

Once you are set up with your Internet access, you can start looking at retail sites you may want to buy from. This is where you need your credit card at the ready. Credit card payment is currently the only viable way to pay for goods online. All the standard credit cards are usually accepted, although you may find that some US sites will accept only American Express. Some sites accept debit cards too, although you need to be aware that you have less legal protection with these than if you use a credit card (see Chapter 3).

What you should see when you open a site

A well-designed site should give you everything you need to know about using the site on its homepage, or at least make it clear to you where to find this information. (The homepage is the page that comes up when you first link to a site.) There should be easy-to-find headings detailing how you order and delivery times and charges. Look in the 'FAQs' (frequently asked questions), 'help' or 'customer service' sections if the relevant information does not seem to be on the homepage.

Good sites are also attractive to look at, with useful photographs, if necessary, and helpful product information.

Ordering your goods

Once you have found a site selling something you would like to buy, the ordering process should be straightforward. The general procedure is more or less the same whatever the site.

When you know which item you want, you simply click on an icon that says 'add to shopping basket' or 'I want to buy' or some such wording. Next you choose how many or what colour or size you want. You will then normally be taken to a page displaying your order and showing the total price including delivery (although some sites do not show this until the very end of the process after you have given your credit-card details). At this point you can choose to go back to shopping if you want more items (the item already in your shopping basket will stay there until you are ready to pay) or click on the icon saying something like 'check out' or 'pay'. Some sites require you to register with them before you order for the first time. You will typically be asked to think of a password and will need to key this in each time you order.

When you are ready to order, you key in your credit-card details, delivery address and email address so that the site can confirm your order. This information will normally be on a 'secure' page – in other words, any information you put on this page will be encrypted or jumbled up when you send it to the retailer so that only the retailer can decipher it. You then click on the 'submit' or 'order' button and that's it – you have made your first online purchase.

After you have ordered

You should get an email from the site confirming your order. This is good practice and all sites should be doing it. If you do not receive an email, ask for one. It is worth printing off emails from the retailer as a paper record of any transaction could come in handy in the event of a dispute.

Sit back and wait for your delivery. Delivery times vary between sites and depend on many factors including what kind of carrier service the site uses. (For example, it may use the mail or a specialist courier service.) Timing can also depend on whether the items you want are in stock and how efficient the site is at organising dispatch. Some retailers spend a lot of money making their site look good but cut corners on the less glamorous delivery service. For standard items in stock, retailers should be able to deliver within a week at the very most. Many promise delivery within two to three days, and some guarantee next-day delivery at no extra charge.

If it looks as if you are going to have to wait longer than expected for your order, the site should email you to let you know. Some sites offer a useful 'order tracking' service so you know exactly at what stage your order is whenever you log on to the site. (For more on delivery, see Chapter 4.)

The best times for shopping

The time of day and day of the week that you choose to do your shopping can affect the speed at which you can shop. This is crucial if you are shopping online in order to save precious time.

The quickest time to shop, especially if you want to do a bit of browsing rather than going straight in and buying, is when there is less 'traffic', which is when other people are less likely to be using the Internet. So that means avoiding traditional business hours (approximately 9 to 5) if you can. Weekends are good, especially first thing in the morning. Alternatively, early morning any day can be quieter and therefore faster. By midday UK time the USA has woken up and is online, so the afternoon is likely to be slower as there are simply more people online.

Finding the shops

2

The Internet, or rather the World Wide Web, can seem like a cyberspace jungle. You might know what you want and you may well have a fair idea of where you can get it, but finding the site is another matter. Once you actually get to a site that sells what you are looking for, you may start to wonder whether you are getting as good a deal on the price as some of the other sites – or 'bricks-and-mortar' shops – are offering.

Fortunately, there are sites that make it easy for you to find the shop and often the price you are after. Shopping guide sites and the shopping sections, or channels, on general information sites can link you to a shop that suits your needs. Price-comparison sites and co-buying schemes can help you find the best price. In addition, if you would like another viewpoint on the product you want to buy or the site you are intending to buy from, 'shoppers' opinion' sites can give you extra guidance.

So where do you start? First, you will need a web site address. If you do not have a specific one, either from word-of-mouth recommendation or one you have read in a review, try using a search engine, for example, **Google.com**, which has a Real Names Index.

Once you get into the site, check that it accepts orders online. Some shops, even chains such as Habitat and Ikea, use their sites as a showcase or shop window rather than a place to buy, so save yourself the time involved in picking and choosing products by looking for a 'shopping basket' heading or icon first.

It is also worth looking at the Web Directory in Part 2. The sites listed there have been included to give you a taste of the shopping possibilities now available on the Internet. We hope this will save you the trouble of wading through the often extremely long lists of sites featured in online shopping directories. Look up the type of product and browse through a selection of sites. In fact, 'browsing' is a key word when it comes to getting familiar with Internet shopping. Just as you would wander through more than one high-street clothes shop, say, in your efforts to find something you like, so trying out (but not necessarily buying from) a range of sites is likely to be more fruitful than sticking to the first one you come across.

Sites that can help you shop

Shopping guide sites which are based on a directory of shops, shopping sections on general information sites, price-comparison, co-buying and opinion sites can all make your experience of shopping on the Net smoother and quicker. Even if the site you are using cannot link you directly to your ideal shop, it should at least be able to point you in the right direction and, in the process, give you some handy information on the product you want.

The Internet is constantly changing, and the differences between the types of shopping site are becoming blurred. Shopping guide sites and shopping sections on general sites, for example, increasingly are offering price-comparison search facilities too. Special shopping schemes such as co-buying (see below) are no longer confined to the specialist sites that originated the ideas, and just about every site has an online auction (see Chapter 6). Sites are linking up, merging, changing names and 'going global'. For the average Internet shopper this means that a single site could well provide for most of your shopping wants and needs. It's just a matter of finding one that suits you.

Shopping sections on general sites

If you are new to Internet shopping and want to get a taste of what it involves, visiting a shopping section on a general information site is a good introduction. These sites are usually referred to as 'portal' sites. They offer a range of features based around a search engine. As well as shopping, you can use the site to keep up with the news and weather, read magazine-style articles on various topics, send emails, enter competitions and talk to other users via chatrooms. The idea behind portal sites is that visitors will find them so useful they will use them as their basic starting point every time they want to do anything on the Internet.

Many ISPs and the bigger search engines run their own portal sites incorporating shopping sections. The shopping sections on these sites vary in what they offer. Some will have just a few 'chosen' retailers within each shopping category. The retailers will have paid for their prime spot on the site. Others provide long lists of retailers and are more like shopping directories. With both, when you click on the retailer's name you go directly through to that site and buy from there rather than the portal site.

Arguably, the portal sites with just a few featured retailers are the easiest and the best to start with. If you are a novice to Internet shopping – and often even when you are an old hand – being presented with a lengthy list of retailers when you are not certain what you want can over-whelm. A list of four rather than 44 shops is more manageable. The other advantage with a smaller selection is that the portal site is more likely to have set criteria, covering matters such as security and customer service, which retailers have to meet before the site links up with them. Check this on the site. The disadvantage is that your choice of retailers is small so if these portals are the only sites you ever use to shop, your Internet shopping experiences are going to be pretty limited. But, again, for the novice they can serve a purpose.

Sites to try

AltaVista.co.uk – a leading search engine; covers the standard shopping categories including home and garden, health and beauty, clothing, music and toys, with 1–4 retailers' sites featured within each. A mixture of high-street names and others. However, be warned that not all the retailers featured were selling online at the time of going to press.

Excite.co.uk – long lists of retailers rather than a select few. Useful if you want to browse more specialist retailer sites. Brief description of each retailer accompanies the listings.

MSN.co.uk – Microsoft's portal site covers a wide range of shopping categories including food and wine, books and lingerie. Choice of 2–8 retailers' sites within each category. Featured retailers include high-street names such as Marks & Spencer and WH Smith. Also separate shopping guides on a range of products.

Yahoo.co.uk – also a leading search engine that is now a portal with a shopping channel. Not the biggest in terms of the shopping categories covered but still useful as an introduction.

Shopping guide sites

These are basically online shopping directories featuring an extensive range of retailers selling just about every kind of product. Products are divided into categories. You click into a category and scroll down the list. Alternatively, you can search by product or shop name. When you find the site you want you click on the name and are linked directly through to it. You buy from the retailer you are linked to rather than the shopping site.

Sites to try

Mytaxi.com – selection of online shops with additional on-site features including a price-comparison facility and a shopping information service where you are emailed with shopping news relevant to you. Also includes a co-buying service (see 'Co-buying sites' below).

Shopsmart.com – one of the largest UK shopping directory sites. Search by category then you are presented with independent assessments (rather than simply summaries) of a huge range of shopping sites. Useful price-comparison feature.

Shopsonthenet.com – established in 1997 (a veteran in Internet terms), this Europe-wide site has over 18,000 retailers in the directory. All the usual shopping categories covered.

The directories on these shopping sites can be excellent sources of information on what's out there. The best will have useful descriptions of each site pointing out relative strengths and weaknesses rather than simply listing the name. Some UK sites will list just UK retailers; others will list a variety of US ones too. The sites often also include shopping articles, product guides and either their own price-comparison search facility or a direct link to a stand-alone price-comparison site (see 'Price-comparison sites' below). The good sites will expect retailers to meet certain requirements regarding, for example, site security before they can be included (for further details see Chapter 3).

The disadvantage of these sites is that although you can discover all sorts of fascinating and unusual shops through them, they can present you with too much information. You might end up viewing long lists of sites before you find anything of interest, although the site's search facilities can be very helpful.

Price-comparison sites

Once you have an idea of what you are looking for, a good price-comparison site can help you find the best price for that product and will include delivery costs in the price to enable you to make a true comparison (although not all the sites do this). You key in your desired product on the site's search facility and a range of prices with direct links to the retailers will be displayed so that you can then go straight to the retailer with the best price. In addition to the dedicated price-comparison sites, a growing number of general shopping sites and shopping directories are incorporating a price-comparison search engine into the site.

The theory behind price-comparison sites is excellent. After all, what more do most shoppers need than a site that can do all the legwork, from providing you with suggestions of products to buy to finding out where they are cheapest and connecting you to that retailer? Price-comparison sites, or good directories featuring price comparisons, could increasingly shape Internet shopping as the sites and the search engines they use become more sophisticated. It is possible that they will become the kingpins of Internet shopping and that retailers' own sites will trail behind because consumers will no longer need to visit them directly.

Price-comparison sites can be very useful, but a lot depends on the type of product you are looking for and how the price search information is displayed. Do not expect price comparisons for every product you could ever want because the sites cannot provide you with this – yet. Instead, many tend to concentrate on key categories. If you are looking for the best deals on CDs, videos and DVDs, computer equipment, software and games, electrical equipment, cameras and books, a price-comparison search could find you the answers you need.

However, even within the same site the quality of information you get varies depending on the product you choose. On one leading site, an 'on-spec' search for a recently released CD by the Irish rock band U2 came up with near-perfect comparative information. Prices, with all shipping costs included, at a range of UK and US retailers were clearly displayed.

Sites to try

Bookbrain.co.uk – specialist price-comparison sites for books. Decent market coverage so there is a fair chance this site will come up with the best deal.

Buy.co.uk – site mainly dedicated to finding the best deals in public utilities. You type in the details of your gas, water or electricity bill and it will come back with the cheapest deal that matches your needs. Also searches for deals for mobile phones, personal loans and credit cards

Dealtime.co.uk – US price-comparison site with a UK wing. It searches US and UK sites and can prove useful if you do not mind buying from non-UK sites. Prices for US sites are displayed in sterling and include shipping charges.

Kelkoo.com – international price-comparison site with the UK wing searching largely UK shops. Price-comparison search covers more categories than some other sites' searches as it includes household appliances, wines and toys.

Pricewatch.co.uk – an interesting site specialising in comparisons on computer hardware and software; also covers other categories such as music, books and financial products

Remember, however, that you need to calculate and include the duty charges for US delivery to get a true price comparison between UK and US sites. (For more information on buying from a non-UK site, see Chapter 5.)

The search for comparisons on a best-selling digital camera was less satisfactory – a reasonable selection of prices were displayed with a 'saving' of £79.99 between the cheapest and most expensive. However, a careful reading of the cheapest retailer's site made it clear that VAT and delivery were not included in the 'display' price, making the saving a much less impressive £12.23.

It is worth bearing in mind that the price comparison you get is often from a limited selection of retailers 'partnered' to the site rather than being a comprehensive hunt of the market. So if you cannot find reasonably impressive savings, try another comparison site or do your own research and see if you can come up with anything better.

Co-buying sites

Co- or group buying is the latest way to shop on the Internet. The idea behind these sites is bulk-buying – hence the more people who register to buy a product, the lower the price can become. The site arranging the co-buy approaches the manufacturer or supplier with a suggested discount price for a specific product. Because so many people will be buying the product, the presumption is that the price will be accepted and the 'co-buy' can go ahead. A time limit of a few weeks is placed on each 'co-buy' and a target price is suggested. A broad range of products are put up by the site for co-buying, from sports bags to computers. Individuals can also suggest products for purchase.

Co-buying can result in real bargains on some products, although it is still worth doing your own price comparisons. The disadvantages are that you have to wait to get your purchase because you are dependent on other co-buyers joining in and you can be restricted in terms of the products available by what other people want.

Sites to try

AltaVista.co.uk – this portal site has a 'group-buying' section in its shopping channel. Reasonable range of products, including an interesting selection in the 'Weird and Wacky' and 'Design Fanatics' sections.

Bluecarrots.com – not a co-buying site as such but one that extols the benefits of co-ownership of the site. You join the site as a club member and become entitled to free shares. The main benefit of being a member is that if you buy from a partnered retailer via the site, you get reductions on goods in the form of cash back. This cash builds up in your own site account and is paid back to you once a year. The reductions available can be quite small, however, and the shopping categories are limited.

Letsbuyit.com – the best-known co-buying site. Wide range of product categories. Co-buyers from all over Europe can take part in the same buys – these multi-country buys tend to reach the best price sooner as more people are involved.

Shoppers' review sites

If you are feeling unsure about which brand of a particular type of product to buy or which online shop to buy it from, you can canvass the opinions of other shoppers via the Internet. Special-interest newsgroups can be very useful for exchanging views. Newsgroups are online public discussion groups organised by topic. You can find one to match your interest by using a search engine, or via the email menu if your ISP gives access to newsgroups. Sites such as **www.deja.com** focus mainly on searching

Sites to try

Epinions.com – reviews from members of the public and professionals on a wide range of products from the latest computers to toys and games. Reviews can be detailed and are arguably more use than simple ratings. Although this is a US site, many of the products are available in the UK so it is still worth a look for shoppers based here. (**Dooyou.co.uk** offers a similar service but is UK-based so products may be more familiar.)

epubliceye.com – US-based site but UK retailers are included in its directory of 'trustworthy' online shops. The theory is that when you buy from a site with a Public Eye logo, you complete an online form rating your experiences. Ratings are given for factors such as customer support and on-time delivery. Public Eye compiles the ratings into a report which is then available to view on its site. Useful extra information on each retailer includes a history of the company's site along with returns policies and security details.

Shopspy.co.uk – UK online shops are reviewed and 'tested' by the site (in the sense that the site has ordered a product from the shops featured). The review includes information on how quickly the product was sent and how well it was packaged, plus details on how long the site has been up and running.

Which.net – Which? Online runs a Which? Web Trader forum where shoppers can exchange views on retailers belonging to the Which? Web Trader oniine shopping code of practice. The scheme covers a significant number of UK online retailers (for more on the code of practice and the benefits to consumers see Part 3). The service is available only to Which? Online subscribers, although non-members who have something to say about a Web Trader can also email their views.

newsgroups. Some online retailers, particularly those dealing in specialist products, may have discussion forums on their sites too. And nowadays sites selling books and music often display reviews by ordinary site-users. **Amazon.com** was one of the first sites to do this.

Entire sites devoted to the exchange of opinions on retailers and products are more common in the USA, but even these can be useful to UK-based shoppers. Remember, though, that these opinions may not always be objective; in theory anyone wanting to promote a certain retailer or product can manipulate the results on these sites. That aside, they can still make interesting reading.

Auction sites

Online auctions have become a very popular form of online shopping. Auctions are well suited to the Internet because shoppers can get involved in a 'chase' for a good deal from the comfort of their homes. But beware, auction sites account for 70 per cent of Internet fraud. Stand-alone auction sites are available as well as auctions on more general sites. New and reconditioned products are auctioned along with second-hand goods and collectables. You buy from the individuals or retailers who put their products up for auction rather than from the site itself. You can find bargains this way but you need to be aware of the legal drawbacks of buying from some auction sellers. Auction sites can also be useful if you have anything to sell. For more on online auctions, see Chapter 6.

Using a search engine

You should be able to find most of the products you could ever want using one, or more likely, a combination of the sites mentioned on pages 31 and 32. But sometimes, particularly if you are looking for an unusual item and do not know the names of any shops likely to sell it, using a general search engine may be the best way of coming up with retailers selling what you need. Search engines look through web pages for titles, words and links and build up a huge index of site profiles. When you type in what you want and press 'search', the search engine looks through this index rather than searching the web 'live'.

The following search engines are straightforward to use for beginners:

Ask Jeeves – www.ask.co.uk
Google – www.google.com
Yahoo! – www.yahoo.co.uk

Make sure you read the search advice on the search engine site before you start. This can save you time and effort looking through lists of irrelevant results. However, do not expect instant perfect results the first time you try. Using a search engine effectively can take practice.

Other search engines are more complicated because you need to use special symbols or words to narrow down your search to get the best results.

Searching on the sites that use symbols and Boolean logic (see box) may take a little practice but it will pay off because these sites could provide the results you are after. If you do not get relevant results from the first search engine you use, try a couple of others. Different search engines search and index varying amounts of the web and will therefore give different results

A quick example of Boolean Logic

You want to buy a new washing machine/tumble drier

You decide to use one of the search engines to get some information on new products.

Carefully wording your search can help you eliminate unwanted information and focus the search on the information you really want.

By keying in:

washing machine* AND tumble drier* you will get sites with information on both (see Example A)

washing machine* OR tumble drier* you will get sites with information on either or both (i.e. loads of information) (see Example B)

washing machine* NOT tumble drier* you will get sites which mention only washing machines (see Example C)

Not all search engines use Boolean logic. AltaVista and Northern Light are two that do.

Notes:
Always use capital letters for AND, OR and NOT
* use this with caution. (For example, car* will find sites which mention cars but also carpets, cardboard etc.)
Remember, always check the Help section or the search tips section of the search engine you choose. They may use some or all aspects of Boolean logic or other search tools.

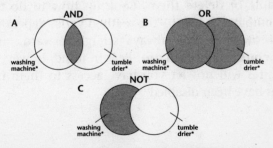

The experienced shopper

Once you get a taste for shopping online, you can tweak your computer and the information you give to various sites in order to personalise your shopping experiences.

Letting the sites get to know you

If you regularly shop at a certain site, that site may keep account of your preferences and alert you to products or special offers coming up that may interest you. Sites do this in a variety of ways. For example, it may ask you to fill in an online questionnaire stating your likes and dislikes. A more efficient way, however, to gather and keep up-to-date with your tastes is to place an identifying file called a 'cookie' on your browser. This cookie gathers information on what products you have been looking at or ordering whenever you visit the site. For example, if you regularly order books or CDs by a certain author or band, the site can deploy the cookie to build up a profile of your tastes and use this to inform you of new publications or releases within your area of interest.

This is clearly useful to the sites because they can market potential purchases to you directly. It can be useful to you too because you do not have to input all your details each time you log on or order and you are able to take advantage of the latest deals and releases. However, if you do not want cookies on your machine, you can reset your browser to disable or delete them. Look up how to do this in your computer manual – the method varies depending on your browser but is always straightforward, or visit **www.cookiecentral.com**. Bear in mind, however, that some sites will not let you have access to them if their cookies have been disabled.

Building your own personal page

Some sites allow you to personalise your link to them. If you visit a site regularly it can be useful to make prominent the information that interests you the most on 'your' site. You can also delete features you never use or read. Bol.com, an Internet bookshop, asks you to select the kinds of books, music or films you like and it creates a MyBol page for you, featuring news and reviews about the titles, authors, directors and artists that are most likely to whet your appetite.

Using special software

Downloading extra software can enhance your shopping, depending on what you are shopping for and whether you want the full experience of all the latest graphics and sounds. You may well already have the latest software installed. If not, you will be able to download the software free via the sites that use it. The site will tell you what you need to use.

If you want to listen to music online or view video clips, you will need the right software. In some ways, the flashier the site, the more irritating it can be, especially if you just want to get down to some simple shopping. Sites that use the latest design innovations will often give you the option of viewing the site at full spec, in which case you can choose to download the appropriate software, or of sticking to their standard viewing format.

Joining loyalty schemes

Just as the supermarkets once competed to encourage shoppers to use loyalty cards, so shopping sites are beginning to embrace this practice. The principle behind any kind of loyalty scheme is basically the same – you, the customer, shop at or simply visit a particular shop or site as much as you can and as a reward receive loyalty points which translate into discounts.

The loyalty schemes UK Internet users are most likely to come across include iPoints (**ipoints.co.uk**) and Beenz (**beenz.com**). Sites pay to be part of these schemes in the hope they can attract custom. With iPoints, for example, when you link to the site you see a directory of retailers which take part in the scheme. The idea is that you choose to visit their sites to amass iPoints. Your iPoints can be saved in your own iPoint account to earn you various treats including days out, products, travel vouchers and flights. It's a bit like a cross between Green Shield Stamps and Air Miles. You can also earn points by completing a customer questionnaire or clicking in to an advert.

Other schemes are a bit different. With **ipledge.net**, for example every time you visit this site and go through them to a 'partner' online shop, that shop donates a percentage of the amount you spend to a charity chosen by you.

You can choose to ignore these loyalty schemes – all you need to do is not register. But if you like the idea of this kind of scheme and are likely to visit lots of sites, building up your loyalty points and exchanging them for 'rewards' could become a new hobby.

Safe, stress-free shopping

3

As a consumer you have the same rights when you buy on the Internet as you have when you buy from mail-order companies or any ordinary shop in the UK. Recent European legislation has further strengthened the position of Internet shoppers so that you have even more protection than before. Although worries about Internet shopping have been exaggerated, this does not mean that buying products on the Internet is always going to be problem-free.

Paying safe

The usual way of paying for goods when shopping on the Net is with a credit or debit card. One of the issues that has concerned prospective Internet shoppers, and prevented some people from using the Internet to shop at all, is the perceived danger of credit-card fraud. This includes being charged for goods that do not turn up and credit-card numbers being intercepted. Some online shoppers have experienced fraud, but in relation to the number of people who use the Net for shopping, such problems are rare.

The reality is that using your credit card to buy goods on the Net or in any 'distance' contract is a very sensible way to shop because of the extra protection you get. In the unusual event that your card details are fraudulently used, you are entitled to cancel any contract and get a refund of any money paid from the card company. You will not be liable for the first £50 of the loss – which you could be if you had used the card in a face-to-face transaction.

Reducing the risks

Although your shopping rights over the Internet are the same as with any other form of shopping when you buy from a UK site, it pays to make some checks on the Internet trader you propose to purchase from before you part with your money. Because of the 'distance selling' nature of the Internet, it is still the case that the few traders who really want to avoid being pinned down can do so fairly easily.

Codes of practice

Checking that the Internet trader follows a recognised online code of practice is an important way of gaining some 'independent' reassurance that the trader is running his or her business according to standards that meet the needs of consumers. Such standards include basic but crucial details such as the trader giving 'real' contact information on the site – in other words, a phone number and address for queries or complaints – and having a proper complaints procedure. (A PO box number does not count.) Several current codes of practice aim to address the particular problems of shopping on the Internet. The Which? Web Trader scheme run by Consumers' Association is probably the best-known (see below). Others are run by industry bodies – the Association of British Travel Agents (ABTA), for example, has one covering the travel industry.

Which? Web Trader

The logo you are most likely to come across on a site is the one showing that the retailer is a Which? Web Trader (see example on page 104). This successful code of practice scheme, run by Consumers' Association, has about 900 retailers (see list in Part 3) as we go to press. The logo indicates that you will be dealing with a legitimate and customer-friendly retailer. Retailers do not pay to be part of the scheme – they are accepted only if their selling policies match the strict criteria set out in the Which? Web Trader Code of Practice. Which? Online carries out random checks to ensure the trader is sticking to the code and removes traders from the scheme if necessary.

Key aspects of the code of practice include:

- full contact details for the retailer should be on the site
- the price of goods and services should be clear and easily found – the price quoted should include any extras such as delivery
- the site must be secure for sending credit-card details, and information on the type and level of security being used on the site should be provided
- customers must be entitled to cancel their orders within 7 days without a reason – the 7 days start from when they receive the goods
- no promotional emails should be sent without the customer's consent
- a clear statement should be displayed when the customer's personal information is being collected saying what it is to be used for
- there should be a fair and effective system for handling complaints.

For fuller details of the Which? Web Trader Code of Practice see Part 3

Ten steps to stre

Unless you know the retailer you are ordering from – maybe through
about or know as a 'bricks-and-mortar' shop – and are reasonal

- **Look for the TrustUK logo.** A trader displaying this logo on
  his or her web site subscribes to an officially recognised code of
  practice which sets high standards of customer service. The
  Which? Web Trader scheme, for example, is backed by TrustUK
  and gives a range of important guarantees about the legitimacy
  and standards of service provided by member traders. If a
  retailer does not display the TrustUK logo it does not mean you
  should avoid buying from that site – many of the best-known
  web retailers are not members of the scheme and still have high
  standards of service. However, the logo affords consumers that
  extra bit of reassurance when purchasing goods from less well-
  known retailers. (For more on TrustUK see page 188)
- **If you have not heard of a company, do some Internet
  research**. Email a relevant news group for opinions. For
  example, if you are interested in buying plants from a
  gardening site and want an independent view on that site, you
  could post a message on a gardening newsgroup (try a
  specialist search engine such as **www.deja.com** to help you
  find a relevant group) or try a search engine such as
  Google.com or one of the shopping directory sites such as
  Shopsmart.com for references.
- **Look for 'real world' contact details**. A telephone
  number and postal address as well as an email address on the
  site show that the company really does exist and is happy to be
  contacted. By law the retailer is obliged to give a postal address
  on his or her site, where it takes money upfront. Be aware that
  just because a site has UK in its web site address, this does not
  mean that it is based in the UK. Check for a UK contact address
  and prices in sterling if you prefer to buy from a UK-based site.
- **Check that the site is secure**. When you are in a secure part
  of a site (usually the page where you give your details), a
  security symbol will appear at the bottom of the screen (in
  Netscape this is a padlock, in Internet Explorer the padlock will
  be closed). Many sites have an encryption facility to scramble

ee shopping

rd-of-mouth recommendation, or a site you have read
nfident about the service provided, it pays to follow this advice.

credit-card details while in transit – aim to shop from these for extra security. The security information should be easy to access on the site. If you are not satisfied that the site is secure, ring the listed phone number and arrange to pay by more conventional means, using the site just as a shop window.

- **Study the web site and email address carefully**. Unscrupulous sellers may make their address as similar as they can to one used by a well-known company by simply adding a couple of letters.

- **Check out the company's privacy policy**. Good traders will have a clear statement on the site telling you how they deal with your personal information. You may need to search around for a site's privacy statement – try looking under 'Terms and conditions', 'Frequently asked questions' or 'Customer service'. If you cannot find any information, email the firm and ask. You should also be able to choose whether to receive future marketing emails from it or third parties.

- **Make sure you know the total amount you are going to be charged.** Check whether the total includes postage and packing and watch out for additional charges such as VAT.

- **Look at delivery times and the refund and returns policy**. Make sure the times given on the site suit you. You are legally entitled to return most goods within seven working days of delivery if they are not what you want.

- **After you have placed your order, make sure you receive a confirmation of that order.** This is a legal requirement. Print out any communications you have with the trader so that you have a paper record of your dealings with it. For extra security, print out a copy of the advert or web page featuring the product you are buying.

- **Check your credit-card statements carefully**. Be extra-vigilant if you have bought from a non-UK web site and prices are quoted in a foreign currency.

TrustUK

Another logo to look out for is the one for TrustUK. This is a non-profit organisation developed by industry bodies and Consumers' Association and is backed by the government. It has been established to provide an official 'hallmark of quality' to sites which follow codes of practice reaching the high standards set by TrustUK.

As the number of retailers selling via the Internet continues to grow, so the likelihood is that codes of practice will proliferate and will vary in terms of the level of protection they offer. There is always the danger that a code of practice can be set up and used more as a marketing tool than to provide a meaningful and worthwhile level of shopping security. This is not helpful for consumers. TrustUK has been put in place to guide consumers towards sites that do have meaningful codes of practice.

You will see the TrustUK logo underneath the Which? Web Trader logo on Which? Web Trader member sites, for example. If you are unhappy with the trader's response to your complaint, you should go to the association or organisation that runs the code of practice to which the trader has signed up. If the problem is still not resolved, you can report the trader and the association to TrustUK.

Sites that do their own checks

The main general shopping directory sites as well as shopping channels that are part of larger web sites are likely to insist on a set of criteria that traders have to meet if they want to be linked to the site. These criteria may not be as legally binding or as stringent as the codes of practice mentioned above but it is useful to know that the traders have been 'checked out' in some way. The criteria for allowing retailers to become site 'partners' should be displayed somewhere on the shopping directory site.

How the law protects online shoppers

Whether or not online traders have customer-friendly policies, they still have to abide by the law. Under UK law, the goods they sell must be of satisfactory quality and fit for their purpose. They should match their description and be safe to use. If they are not, you are legally entitled to claim your money back, provided you act quickly. If you have paid by credit card, you can claim your money back from the credit-card company if the goods cost between £100 and £30,000, as well as from the trader. Credit-card payment also covers you for consequential loss – for example, if the toaster you have bought is faulty, catches fire and damages your kitchen work-top, you can claim the cost of repairs to the work-top from the credit card company, if the loss is over £275.

Recent European legislation has strengthened and clarified the law relating specifically to 'distance selling' – a term which covers selling via the Internet as well as traditional mail-order or telephone selling. In the UK it is called the Consumer Protection (Distance Selling) Regulations 2000.

The new law gives you the following rights:

- the right to receive clear information about goods and services before you decide to buy
- confirmation of this information in writing when you buy
- a cooling-off period of 7 working days in which you can withdraw from the contract (this does not apply to certain categories of goods including food and flowers or to CDs, videos or DVDs that have been opened)
- protection from credit-card fraud – credit-card companies are legally obliged to reimburse you if your credit-card details are fraudulently used.

Buying from a non-European Union site can be more complicated if something goes wrong as different laws may apply. Policies vary between card issuers and many argue that they are not liable for overseas purchases. In practice, most will consider claims for up to the value of the purchase. They will not necessarily pay for consequential loss, however. It is worth reading the small print of your credit card agreement carefully. For more on buying from abroad, see Chapter 5.

When things go wrong

Your rights concerning goods bought via the Internet are broadly the same as if you had bought them from a high-street shop.

Faulty goods

If your goods arrive and you are unhappy with them because they are faulty or damaged or simply not as described on the site, notify the seller as soon as possible. You are entitled to get your money back or, if you choose, have a replacement. Give the seller all the relevant information you can, including the date of your order, order number, amount paid and method of payment, the reason for your complaint and how you would like your claim resolved. Put the complaint in writing to the head office if necessary and keep copies of letters and emails, and notes of telephone conversations. The same basic rules apply if you have used the Internet to buy a service – for example, using a travel company to buy a holiday via the Internet. Remember, too, that you have extra protection if you buy using a credit card because you can make a claim against the credit card company rather than the seller.

If you are unhappy with the way the seller is dealing with your complaint, check to see whether he or she is a member of a trade association and approach that association. If the Which? Web Trader or the TrustUK logo is displayed on the web site, these organisations can also get involved (click on the logo on the site for instant access). If you feel your complaint has still not been fairly resolved, approach your local Trading Standards department. The address and phone number will be in the phone book under your local authority or you can find it via the Internet by visiting **www.tradingstandards.gov.uk** and entering your postcode.

You can also get detailed online advice from the following web sites:

- **www.adviceguide.co.uk** (connects to the National Association of Citizens Advice Bureaux)
- **www.oft.gov.uk** (the Office of Fair Trading)
- **www.consumer.gov.uk** (the Department of Trade and Industry's 'Consumer Gateway' web site)

If you are unhappy with the description of a product given in an advert on a web site you can also complain to the Advertising Standards Authority (ASA). Adverts on Internet sites are covered by the British Codes of Advertising and Sales Promotion, which are administered by the ASA and which require all adverts to be 'legal, decent, honest and truthful'. ASA guidelines cover only UK sites and do not cover claims made on companies' own sites.

If your order is not delivered

Unless you have agreed a longer time, the goods must be delivered or the services performed within 30 days of your order. If this does not happen, you can cancel the order and get your money back.

Buying financial products

Anyone setting up a business selling financial services has to be authorised to do so. The Financial Services Authority (FSA) regulates some financial service businesses in the UK. There are certain checks you can make before dealing with a company selling these services. These include:

- check that the company is authorised. Call the Financial Services Authority's Public Enquiries Office (0845 606 1234) to confirm this, or contact the FSA via its web site at **www.fsa.gov.uk** Don't just take the company's word for it.
- if you are dealing with a financial services company based in another part of the European Union, you can contact the Public Enquiries Office to check that the company is entitled to undertake the specific financial service you require in the UK.

Junk emails or 'spam'

Junk or unsolicited emails (known as 'spam') are, broadly speaking, commercial messages sent to you without your permission. They may be from companies you have dealt with before or from those with which you have had no previous contact – these will have bought your email address from a list broker along with thousands of other addresses. The emails may be irritating rather than harmful. But fraud-sters have used them to entice people into scams.

It is usual for you to give your email address when you buy something on the Internet. Traders use it to send confirmation of your order to you. But there is the risk that an unscrupulous trader may pass your address on to other parties without your permission. If this happens, you could find yourself at the receiving end of a barrage of unwanted emails.

Putting a stop to unwanted emails

Just because you give your email address to a company, it does not mean you will start getting unsolicited emails. In fact, in a survey by Which? Online, Internet shoppers did not find unsolicited emails a problem. If unsolicited emails have become an issue for you, however, there are steps you can take:

- if you know the source of the email, ask the sender to stop sending them. If they do not stop or if you cannot tell the source, ask your ISP if it can put a block on future emails from that sender
- spot the emails before you download them. When emails are sent in bulk to lots of addresses at the same time, your name often will not appear on the 'To' line of these emails. Instead, you are sent as a 'Blind Copy' (BC) recipient of the mailing. In addition, the address on the 'To' line may be identical to the address on the 'From' line
- check online retailers' privacy statements before you buy. Aim to buy only from those traders who guarantee not to pass your details on.

From mouse to house: delivery

4

The delivery side of Net shopping can be impressively efficient or irritatingly cumbersome depending on the site you are ordering from, how the goods are delivered and whether or not you are likely to be at home to receive them. It's fair to say that most goods will be delivered without a hitch but you may encounter some hiccups if you regularly order from a range of sites.

Delivery times

Always check the delivery details on the site – a good site will have them clearly displayed. Different retailers present these details in different ways. Some sites display a maximum time to cover themselves in case of difficulties, so even though the one you order from shows a comparatively long time for delivery, say 14 to 28 days, you will more than likely receive your order much sooner. How soon you receive your goods will also depend on whether the site is UK based. (For fuller information on buying from non-UK based sites, see Chapter 5.)

Many sites can arrange next-day delivery for you at extra cost. Some sites guarantee next-day delivery at no extra charge, although they may stipulate that you have to order by a certain time of day. If the delivery information on any site is unclear, email or telephone the company for clarification.

Delivery charges

These can vary from site to site and depend on the type of product and quantity you are ordering. Unfortunately, many sites do not always make delivery charges immediately clear, so you may have to search around for the details. Try the 'Frequently asked questions', 'Information' or 'Customer service' headings. On some sites the cost is calculated towards the end of the ordering process. On a few sites, you have to key in your credit-card details as well before the delivery charge becomes clear. This can be irritating if all you want is to find out exactly how much you have to pay before you decide to order. Remember, though, that even if you have to do this, it is only when you click the final 'Place order' button that your credit card details go through.

Some sites offer free delivery. However, this does not always work out cheaper. These sites may cover themselves for postage in the displayed price which could be higher than the total price on another site that does make a delivery charge. As always, if you are after the best price, it pays to shop around, making sure you look at the total price whether or not there is a delivery charge.

Means of delivery

How will your goods be delivered? Some sites use courier companies but many tend to use standard post or Parcelforce services.

The postal service has some practical advantages. First, the post often arrives in the early morning so you are more likely to be around to receive your goods. Second, if you are not at home, you can get goods re-delivered or you can collect them from the local sorting office (which tends to be open in the early morning). And third, the postal service also delivers on a Saturday.

Courier services can be fast and efficient but most deliver only during the day Monday to Friday so you may have to make special arrangements to stay at home to receive your package. If you are out, most courier companies will leave a card saying that they can deliver at a more convenient time for you, but you must ring them to arrange a time.

Open the box

One possible solution if you order a lot of goods via the Internet but are often not at home during the day to receive the delivery is to have a specially designed secure box outside your home. Such 'box schemes' are still at the experimental stage but they could be the way forward for deliveries, and pilot schemes are up and running.

There are two types of possible boxes at the time of writing – temporary and permanent. With the first, the company can deliver your goods in a secure box and leave it outside your home with your goods inside. When you get in from work, you take out your shopping and the box is removed by the retailer or delivery company the next day.

Alternatively, a box could be installed permanently outside your home. Whenever you have a delivery, it would be placed inside the box ready for you to collect. Both types of box would be securely attached to your home either to a cable so that the box can be detached and taken away after you have taken out your order or on a permanent fixture. Supermarket deliveries are the most obvious type of goods that could benefit from a box system, but most products from books to dry-cleaning can be 'boxed' in this way.

Obviously security is an issue here. With the current temporary box scheme, a metal panel is bolted to the outside of your house. This panel holds three 'ports' to which the cables that secure the delivery boxes can be attached. You can use a swipe card to release the cable and open the box.

For the permanent box, you use a lock and key. This is electronically linked to a central control room. The people making the deliveries are given an access code to tap into the box to open it – the code is unique to each delivery. See **www.bearbox.com** and **www.homeporthome.com** for more details on experimental schemes running at the time of writing.

Checking your order and returning unwanted goods

Some sites offer an 'order tracking' service so you can check if your order has left the depot. You type in your order or customer number and can find out at what stage in the delivery process your order has reached. Whether or not a site offers this service, it is good practice for a site to email you once your order has been dispatched.

What happens when your goods arrive but you decide you do not want them? Most companies' web sites will take them back and refund your money, but beware, the company can charge additional costs. You usually have to pay the postage costs for returning the item. The site may also charge a handling fee for accepting back unwanted goods. Look carefully at the site's returns policy before you order.

Web sites that delivered by mail rather than courier came out better in a *Which?* survey – see *Which?* November 2000.

Buying from abroad

5

The ability to choose and buy products from abroad easily and quickly is one of the most exciting prospects of shopping on the Internet. Before online shopping, buying from abroad tended to be limited to holidays and business trips or for non-travellers, pricey international phone calls and possibly time-consuming payment and delivery procedures. Nowadays, if you want to buy a CD not yet available in the UK or to browse a US clothes store, you can do it within minutes.

Goods such as CDs and computer equipment can be cheaper abroad, although you should still make price comparisons with UK retailers. Prices will be quoted in foreign currencies so you will need to convert (for more on currency converters, see page 58). You may also need to budget for custom and delivery charges. This is discussed later in this chapter.

For other products, the attraction of buying from abroad is not so much to make major savings but to get hold of items not available in the UK – books which are published only in the USA, for example.

However, buying from abroad can give rise to additional problems if you are not happy with the goods you have ordered or if they do not turn up. The laws of another country may apply, and pinning down a slippery retailer thousands of miles away may not be the easiest of tasks. Be very aware of mounting costs. That fantastic deal may not be quite so impressive once delivery costs, customs duty and VAT have been added.

Where to look and what to look for

The USA is very popular with UK online shoppers and browsers who like the idea of buying from abroad. This is partly because the sites are in English but also because the USA has tended to be a few steps ahead in Internet terms with more innovations, more sophisticated sites and more product choice than anywhere else. Computer and electronic goods, CDs and books are the main categories with a reputation for good deals.

It is fair to say, however, that UK-based sites are making great strides to catch up. Existing online retailers have responded to the competition, and new UK sites, often based on successful US models, have been springing up. American sites have also been 'going global' at a fast rate – many have now opened up UK 'branches'. Competition between UK sites has intensified and this has had a positive impact on prices. CDs are generally cheaper in the USA but may be the same price or cheaper in the UK, when delivery costs and customs charges are taken into consideration.

So what does all this mean to shoppers keen to take up the much-hyped prospect of bargain deals abroad? Basically, it underlines that you should check out UK prices too if the product you are after is available. Do not presume that it will automatically be cheaper in the USA. You need to do your homework first. Even taking into consideration the fact you do not have to pay duty on some goods you buy from abroad – computers, for example – delivery costs and sometimes the prospect of lengthy delivery times can make the whole prospect less attractive.

Finding the sites

It can still be well worth looking at sites based abroad, particularly when it comes to specialist items that may be impossible to get in the UK. For example, you know what you want and you have heard that you can get cheap deals on that product in the USA but you do not know any specific US sites nor how to start finding them.

Your first step could be to try out one of the many US price-comparison sites. This can save you the time and effort involved in checking out sites listed in an online directory. Look at more than one of these sites – this will also help you to get familiar with retailers' names and the kinds of deals they offer. The price-comparison sites listed below are among the best-known.

Sites to try

Bottomdollar.com deals in the standard products that most price-comparison sites cover such as books, computing and electrical equipment but also offers price comparisons on a wide range of other items including fragrances and fashion. A UK branch of the site deals in a smaller range of products

Dealtime.com (this also has a UK branch which compares UK and US prices for some products)

Mysimon.com comparison site covering a similarly broad range of products as BottomDollar but arguably more user-friendly. The site offers comparisons for products at more than 2,000 online stores and aims to provide product availability and shipping information with the items it lists. You can also access their sites in France and Germany, but no UK site at the time of writing.

You could also try out a US site called **TopTenLinks.com** This is a general-interest Internet directory containing the top ten sites in a wide range of product categories. The site is useful because it offers only the names of high-profile, leading sites. It also lists price-comparison sites.

In some cases, even though a UK branch of a US site may have the same name, the choice of products may not be as extensive as on the US site. So if you know that a site you like has a US base, it can be worth investigating the US site to see what it offers.

Once you have found the US retailer's site, you will want to convert the display price into sterling (remember to include delivery charges). To make an accurate conversion into sterling you can use one of the many currency converters available on the Internet. Some sites have their own in-built currency converters. Or try the Universal Currency Converter (**www.xe.com/ucc**) or the converter on the *Financial Times*' site, **ft.com.** However, the exchange rate you will pay on your credit card will vary daily.

Checking delivery charges

Before you order, look for the shipping information. Sites that encourage international orders should make international delivery costs clear. You will often be offered a choice of speedy courier-style delivery, which can take a matter of days, or a much slower service which is cheaper but can take some weeks. For example, one leading US computer site gives a delivery quote for a computer printer of $40 (£30 or so) for delivery to the UK in three working days. A US music site quotes air-mail charges of $10 (£7) for between one and three CDs which the site says can take several weeks to deliver, or $25 (approx £18) for the much quicker Federal Express service. This is how it *should* work and indeed does with many sites.

Ordering and paying

However, all too often you will find a site that seems to offer an excellent deal, only to discover once you go to key in your order that the retailer does not deliver to customers abroad. Even if a site says it will accept international orders, it is not always an easy process. Some sites do not accept credit cards issued outside the USA. Others might accept only American Express cards. The site may say you can wire the money or send travellers cheques but then you do not get the legal benefits that you do when you pay with a credit card (see Chapter 3). One US site selling digital cameras asks international customers to fax a photocopy of both sides of their credit card to them. This is hardly shopping at the press of a button.

With sites that do not make it easy for you to pay online, you may be better off voting with your mouse and moving on to a site that is more hospitable towards international customers. It is also prudent to check a site's delivery policies as soon as you visit the site rather than leaving it until the end.

Paying duty and VAT

Delivery charges are not the end of it. The general rule is if you are buying from outside the European Union you are liable to pay duty and VAT on goods you order in. If you buy from another country in the EU you do not have to pay duty but you do have to pay VAT.

As always, there are exceptions to the rule:

- imports of less than £18 (including post and packing) are free from duty and VAT
- computers, computer parts and digital still cameras are free from duty. Books are free from duty and VAT (so buying these products from abroad can be especially cost-effective, despite delivery costs)
- alcohol, tobacco or perfumes are always liable for duty and VAT, the goods may be confiscated if neither duty nor VAT are paid.
- digitised products such as software and music clips that you order and download directly on to your computer are regarded by Customs and Excise as 'services' rather

than products, so are free from duty (but they are liable for VAT, although this is rarely collected).

How much do you need to pay?

VAT is normally 17.5 per cent (for antiques it is 5 per cent). The amount of duty you pay depends on the product you are buying. For example:

- CDs carry a duty of 3.5 per cent
- CD players, 9 per cent
- clothes, 12.8 per cent
- DVD players, 14 per cent
- ski boots, 17 per cent.

For a list of common items and the duty rates that apply, go to the duty section of the Customs and Excise web site (**www.hmce.gov.uk/bus/regions/dutyrate.htm**). If you cannot see the product you are interested in listed, ring Customs and Excise advice service on 020-7202 4227 to find out the rate.

Once you have found the rate simply multiply the purchase price (including any local taxes) by the Duty Rate percentage and this will give you the amount of duty to be paid. The amount of VAT you pay on a product is calculated from the total price *including* the duty. Multiply the total of the purchase price and the duty charge by the VAT percentage – normally 17.5 per cent – and this will give you the amount of VAT you have to pay.

Customs and Excise gives an example on its web site of how to calculate duty and VAT if you buy £100-worth of CDs.

The duty rate on CDs is 3.5% and the VAT 17.5%.
3.5 % x £100 = £3.50 (This is the duty)
£100 + £3.50 = £103.50 x 17.5% (i.e. the VAT rate) = £18.11 (the VAT you pay)
Total duty and VAT to pay = £3.50 + £18.11 = £21.61.

How the charges are collected

The supplier has to put a special label on any international package. This indicates to Customs and Excise the contents of the package and how much it is worth. The package will be opened only if the label is missing or unclear. Customs then add the extras you need to pay. The Post Office or the delivery company will collect the duty and VAT from you on behalf of Customs and Excise when it delivers the package to you. There is a charge for doing this – the Parcelforce fee for standard deliveries is currently £5.10. However, a Which? Online survey showed that charging is a little haphazard and many shoppers escape paying duty and VAT because the charge is not collected when their parcel arrives.

Making sure you get the goods you want

Apart from checking the final price, including all the extras, it pays to make some further checks before parting with your credit-card number:

- make sure electrical equipment will work in the UK – different standards and systems can apply in other countries so ask the supplier to confirm that the product is UK-compatible
- check out the guarantee – make sure it is valid in the UK and find out whether the goods have to be returned to the supplier's country if something goes wrong or whether you can use an affiliated dealer in the UK
- be wary when buying videos from abroad – US and Japanese videos are NTSC format and cannot be played in the UK. Some sites do sell VHS but you need to check with them. There may also be problems with DVDs. Again, check with the site.

Taking precautions

It pays to be extra-vigilant when buying from a web site abroad because of the greater potential for problems. Remember, too, that although it is still best to pay by credit card because of the extra protection you get, credit card companies may not be quite as customer-friendly if you have bought something from outside the EU and something goes wrong as they have to be when it comes to reimbursing you for a product bought within the EU. Some companies argue that they are not liable for overseas purchases, although in practice most will consider claims for up to the value of the purchase.

Another useful precaution to take is to check to see whether other people say anything negative about a particular site by looking at one of the 'shoppers opinion' style sites. Try **epubliceye.com** or **Epinions.com** The Internet Consumer Assistance Bureau at **www.isitsafe.com** is a US site that aims to encourage consumer 'policing' of the Internet. If you are concerned about ordering from a particular US site, the Bureau can check out the legitimacy of the retailer for you.

If things do go wrong

If you are not happy with the way things are going try to sort out the matter with the seller first. Recent EU legislation means that you have increased protection against retailers based in the EU. If the seller is based outside the European Union and is not co-operating with you, it may prove more complicated to resolve your concerns. Cross-border disputes can still be fraught with difficulties not least because of delays due to distance and language problems.

However, a number of organisations can give you advice and assistance:

- your local Citizens Advice Bureau – you can get the details from the web site at **www.nacab.org.uk**
- the Office of Fair Trading (OFT) does not get involved in individual complaints but can provide general advice and pass on suitable complaints to associated organisations overseas who may be able to help. Write to the Office of Fair Trading, International and UK Liaison, Consumer Affairs Division, Fleetbank House, 2-6 Salisbury Square, London EC4Y 8JX or visit the Buying from Abroad section of its web site at **www.oft.gov.uk/html/shopping**
- the Advertising Standards Authority (ASA) can help if you feel you have been misled by the way a product has been advertised on the Internet by a European-based site. The ASA is a member of an alliance of European advertising regulatory bodies and can liaise with the appropriate organisation in the relevant European country to try to resolve the complaint. The ASA's web site address is **www.asa.org.uk**
- Consumers' Association has arrangements with consumer organisations in other countries so that Web Trader schemes similar to the Which? scheme (see Part 3) are Europe-wide. Similar schemes have so far been set up in Belgium, France, Italy, the Netherlands, Portugal and Spain. If you have a problem with a trader based in one of these countries and that trader displays the Web Trader logo on the site, you can email the Which? Web Trader scheme at *webtrader@which.net* for advice on what to do.

Online auctions

6

Online auction sites are very popular and are becoming more so as increasing numbers of people choose to shop on the Internet. It is worth logging on to an auction site because it can be so entertaining to witness the electronic wheeler-dealer process in action (as well as to see some of the more bizarre items up for auction).

If you have something to sell, whether it is an old sofa, a collection of unwanted CDs or a valuable rare edition of a book, an auction site gives you an electronic forum for your sale and enables you to reach thousands of potential buyers. If you want to buy, you have a good chance of getting what you want for a reasonable price with minimal effort. For those looking for specialist items such as sporting memorabilia or cult TV programme merchandise, auction sites provide an accessible and fruitful alternative to buying from specialist shops, fairs or conventions.

Auction sites also provide retailers with a convenient way of getting rid of excess stock. Some of the items put up for sale by companies or by the site itself (as opposed to individuals) will be on the auction site because they would not sell as easily in the high street. This does not mean the items are defective or worthless, indeed auction sites can often be the homes of the best bargains.

You need to keep your wits about you, however, when you use auction sites because you do not have the same degree of legal protection as when you buy from an ordinary online shop. If something goes wrong with the item you have bought, or if you feel it was misrepresented on the auction site, getting your money back could prove difficult, particularly if you have bought from a private seller (for more on online auction shopping rights, see page 74).

How online auctions work

Broadly speaking, all auction sites operate in the same way. However, they can vary over things such as the nature of the goods you can buy, the type of seller you buy from (a private individual seller, a retailer 'partnered' with the site or from the site operating as a retailer itself) and the general look and user-friendliness of the site.

Looking at what's on offer

When you open an auction site, you will see a list of categories showing the kinds of products you can bid for. Many sites will have a very wide range of categories covering every type of product from footballs to freezers. A few will be much more specialised, dealing in just one broad category – art and antiques, say – which will be divided into sub-categories.

Typically you will be able to browse without registering. If you want to bid, however, you will need to register and give your credit card details. You can look at the items on offer by opening up a category that interests you, or you can search for a specific product using the site's search engine. When the item you have chosen comes up there will often be a photograph next to the description,

---

WARNING

It has been estimated that 70 per cent of all Internet fraud occurs on auction sites. For useful tips and information on how to avoid this go to **www.fraud.org**

---

although these pictures can vary in quality so are not always helpful.

Making a bid

To bid for an item you like, you must offer a price higher than the latest price displayed. (Remember that you must have registered to bid.) Other people who have logged on to the site and also want that item will try to outbid you. And so it goes on. The auction site sets a time limit (with **eBay.co.uk** it is 3, 5, 7 or 10 days). The bidder can see the time until the auction finishes displayed in days and hours. Whoever has offered the highest bid when that time limit expires is notified by the auction company that he or she has won. Items up for auction tend to have a reserve price so this has to be met before a product is sold. You are unlikely to be told what the reserve price is.

Even if you are the highest bidder, you may not have to pay as much as your final bid. On many sites you can set a maximum bid straight away to save you having to log on to see the progress of the bidding all the time. The site then automatically bids for you in your absence, increasing your bid in set increments – say £10 – each time it is matched by someone else. If the other bids have fallen well short of your maximum bid after the time limit is up, you simply pay an increment over the next highest bid rather than the value of your maximum bid.

If you do not opt for the automatic bidding service, keeping track of your bid is made easier by the fact that sites tend to email you when someone else bids higher than you. Many users prefer to log on regularly to follow the bidding and feel part of the online auction experience.

Timing

Bidding can be slow at the start of auctions, speeding up rapidly as the time limit for an auction draws to an end. So do not presume that because you have held the highest bid for a while, you will win. In fact, last-minute bidding has become quite an art form for die-hard auction site users. There is always the chance that nipping in at the very last minute can net you a bargain. Sites may encourage this by highlighting the auctions with only hours to spare before the deadline.

In reality, bidders who have opted to set a maximum bid and use the site's automatic bidding service will win anyway if their maximum bid is higher than yours, even if you got in at the eleventh hour. For auctions for popular items at least, price is more important to winning than timing.

Winning

If your bid is the winning one, the site will contact you to let you know you have won or you will be contacted by an individual seller. If you are buying directly from the site, your credit card will be debited and the goods sent on. If you are buying from an individual seller, you will need to sort out payment and delivery details with that individual.

Taking precautions

Online auctions can be fun (even addictive) and can be the source of real bargains. But it pays to be careful and to do a bit of background research before you order.

Check out the information on the site

Good auction sites are full of information about how best to use them and the kinds of safeguards you should make. They will also have clear contact details in case you need to talk to them directly. If a site seems to be 'holding back' in any way, it may be wiser not to use it.

Find out about extra charges

The delivery charge may not be included in the winning price. Check that the price you see includes VAT. The site should make clear what the delivery charges are – **QXL.com**, for example, one of Europe's leading auction sites charges between £3.95 and £29.99, depending on the weight of the item.

If you are buying from a private seller, you will need to arrange delivery directly with him or her, although you can often pay to use a courier service arranged by the site. If you are buying directly from the site, your item will be delivered to you by that site and you will be charged accordingly. The seller is normally the one who has to pay commission to the site, but some auction sites take a general arrangement fee or premium from the final buyer as well as the seller.

Compare prices elsewhere

Just because a site is an auction site does not mean all items will be at bargain prices. Although many items will not be generally available in the shops, some will be. If the item you want is advertised on the site as brand new and is available in the high street or from other online retailers, it pays to make some price comparisons to get a good idea of the true value before you start bidding. Use one of the price-comparison sites for speedy results (see pages 28–30). And remember that the starting price of auctions will be deliberately low to encourage people to start bidding. However, this does not mean that the selling price will always be low too.

Check out the seller

This is especially important when you are dealing with an independent seller. You do not want to get involved in doing a deal with someone who is going to back out or try to run off with your money. The sites can help you. If the seller has sold anything on the site before, past buyers can give their verdict. This will be in the form of ratings or comments or a combination of both. Higher ratings indicate the seller has responded quickly to requests for information, has provided an accurate description of the goods and has fulfilled any delivery commitments. Sellers with low ratings can be barred from using the site. Useful as this can be, there have been cases of these ratings being falsified. If you are new to online auctions, it may be best to stick to items sold by the site owners, or buy from people who have been recommended by someone you know.

eBay.co.uk, one of the biggest auction sites, automatically reimburses buyers up to £120 (minus the £15 excess e.Bay charge) if the seller fails to hand over the item after payment but NOT if the seller has received overall negative feedback before.

If the seller has never sold on the site before, you can still do some checks. Start off by emailing him or her. A quick response to your queries and open and constructive information on the item are encouraging signs. Ask for a real address and phone number. You could also request online references via email – in other words, any email addresses of people to whom he or she has sold before.

Make sure payments are secure

As with any web site, you should not give your credit card details to an auction site unless you are satisfied the site is bona fide and has secure payment systems (for more on this see pages 42–3). Of course, when you make payments to individuals you are more vulnerable to exploitation. Many sites offer an 'escrow service' which is designed to ensure that payment is made only after the buyer has confirmed that the goods have been received. The usual procedure is that the buyer pays by credit card into an escrow account and the auction site tells the seller that the money is there. The seller then sends the goods and the buyer tells the auction site when they arrive. The seller can then have access to the money.

If there is a problem with the goods, the buyer tells the site and sends them back to the seller. The money stays in the account until the seller confirms the goods have been returned. It is sensible to use such a service if the site offers it as it gives you a bit more protection in an area where Internet shoppers are more vulnerable. The site will normally charge extra for this – QXL's 'Safebay' service is 5 per cent of the final auction price, with a minimum fee of £4.

Getting the online auction bug

Some auction site devotees treat bidding as a hobby and have spent time and effort 'fine-tuning' their auction-buying skills and tactics.

In the USA online auction fever is more ferocious than in the UK. Online auctions have been going for longer, and the range of sites running is much wider, from the mega-successful such as eBay, which now has a truly international user base, to small, community-based 'garage-sale' style sites selling little more than bric-a-brac.

There are even web sites that have been set up by auction fans to exchange views, news and tactics. Auction fans who regularly use different sites can register with sites that act as a kind of 'auction manager' by keeping track of bids on different sites, co-ordinating payment and shipping, and alerting users to auctions that suit their particular interest. **Auctionwatch.com** and **Bidstream.com** are two such sites, both US-based.

Sites with a difference

Art, antiques and collectables, computers and software, books and music and electrical equipment form the mainstay items on most sites. They are generally auctioned off in the same way – in other words, with the buyers competing against each other in a race to get the best price. But a few sites do things differently.

Reverse bidding

You can take part in what is commonly termed 'reverse bidding' on some sites. You, as the bidder, name your price for a product or service and the site gets back to you to let you know whether your 'bid' has been accepted by the seller. **Priceline.co.uk** is the main reverse bidding site. Based in the USA, it now has a UK branch. Bidding on airline flights, hotel rooms and car rentals is available. The theory is that hoteliers, for example, will be willing to rent out their rooms at a cut price if those rooms would otherwise go empty.

Ybag.com, a UK site, operates on the same principle, but you can name your price on virtually any product you choose from cars to baby equipment. You tell the site what you want and what you are prepared to pay and the site will find out if there is a seller to take up your offer. Sensible rather than silly price offers will get results.

At **Reverseauction.com**, a US site, a slightly different auction technique prevails. Prices are set by the seller and drop 'live' on screen until someone buys. Once there is a committed buyer the auction ends.

Live auctions

Live/real-time auctions, where TV pictures of the activity in a real-world auction house are transmitted to your PC or TV screen, are becoming popular.

Theauctionchannel.com, a UK site specialising in information on traditional as well as Internet auctions, offers this service. You use the site to find televised auctions of interest to you. To bid, you need to register with the auction house running the auction. You can then bid live by clicking on a 'bid' icon on your screen as the auction is running. If you win the auction, you will see the auctioneer announcing that you have won. **QXL.tv** is another site running this kind of auction.

Swaps

Many mainstream sites run 'swap shops' as a small part of their service. These give the site a kind of community feel. **Swopworld.com** is a dedicated UK swapping site. You register what you want to swap and say what you would like to swap it for. Alternatively, you can let another user suggest a swap or you can suggest a cash alternative. Computer games, sports and concert tickets and books are common items put up for swap. No money changes hands online – you deal directly with the swapper after you have seen his or her offer.

Specialist sites

In the UK, auction sites are still fairly general in nature and deal with a broad range of categories. In the USA, however, small specialist auction sites seem to blossom alongside the mega-sites. Highly esoteric in nature, many are worth looking at if only for curiosity's sake.

If you want to get a real taste of the range of strange items for sale on some auction sites, pay a visit to **www.disturbingauctions.com**, a site dedicated to the research and study of the most bizarre items for sale on Internet auction sites. The blurb on the site succinctly states: 'one person's trash is another's treasure. But some-times trash is just trash' and goes on to say they search for 'truly tacky stuff that people really, honestly, believed that someone would (and in some cases *did*) buy'. Items are categorised into sections with titles such as 'Emotionally Scarring Toys' and 'Terrifying Dolls'.

More unusual auction sites

- **americangolfauction.com** – for golf and golf-related merchandise
- **aquabid.com** – for everything to do with fish from the fish themselves to aquariums, fish food and fish-themed merchandise
- **gsaauctions.gov** – for US federal government surplus property from commonplace items such as office furniture through to lab equipment, fire trucks and aircraft
- **wrestlingauction.com** – for wrestling collectables including, when we looked, a 16-foot wrestling ring priced at $2,000.

Your rights when using auction sites

You have fewer legal rights when buying at auction sites. Internet companies operating as auctioneers can legally refuse to accept responsibility for the quality of the goods they auction. They present themselves as intermediaries who arrange the sale.

In reality, however, the main auction sites tend to give some sort of guarantee – for example, **QXL.com** states that you can return goods within 14 days if you are not satisfied (although this does not apply if you are buying from private sellers rather than from the site itself or retailer 'partners' of the site), and eBay has a form of free insurance for buyers against sellers not sending goods after payment.

Read the conditions of sale carefully to see what kinds of extra guarantees the site makes before you commit yourself to a sale. You may decide that the risks outweigh the benefits. If you buy from a private seller via an auction site, you may end up with goods with a fault, but as long as they have not been misleadingly described by the seller your legal rights are very limited.

Selling at auctions

Anyone can put up anything (within reason) to sell on an auction site. Most sites have lists of items they will not sell (see box for more details).

What some sites will not sell

eBay's list of restricted items is divided into 'Prohibited' and 'Questionable'. 'Prohibited' includes firearms, fireworks, animals and animal parts, human parts and remains, lock-picking devices, police badges, drug paraphernalia, and descramblers. 'Questionable' objects include 'adults-only' items, autographed items, Nazi memorabilia, used medical devices and batteries.

Yahoo also runs an auction site and its list is much less specific but includes alcoholic beverages, unroadworthy motor vehicles, firearms, offensive weapons and Nazi memorabilia.

Once you decide to sell something on an auction site, the process is relatively straightforward. You need to have registered on the site so that you have a member ID number and a personal password. Next you fill in an online application form, specifying what you have to sell and the most appropriate product category for it to appear in. Give a clear and accurate description of your item, keeping it as brief as you can. Be careful to avoid making a misleading statement about your item – you are legally liable for the description of the product and if it does not do what you say it does, or is not in the condition you claim for it, you could face a claim from the buyer for breach of contract. You need to key in the price at which you want the bidding to start (the lower the better) and also a reserve price, which is the minimum price you are willing to sell the item for. In addition, you must specify delivery and payment details, i.e. the kind of payment you are willing to accept and the likely cost of delivery, if the bidder is to pay for this.

Providing a photograph of the item for sale is not compulsory, but it will help if you want to attract the maximum number of bidders. Try to get a clear, good-quality photograph. This may seem an obvious bit of advice but if you take a look at many of the pictures that appear on the sites, you will see that many sellers think any old photo will do. If you plan to take your own photos, you will need a scanner or digital camera so that you have an image that can be submitted to the site via your computer. Alternatively, you can link to a picture already on the Internet (it may not be necessary to show specifically your own product, as long as you make this clear) – the site will tell you how to do this.

Once you have submitted your application form and it has been accepted by the site, it is posted on the site and you can view it at any time. If you want to know the latest bid status of your auction, the site can email you or you can look at your own account page to see how many bids you have. You will be sent an email when your auction closes along with details of the winning bidder.

You may be charged a fee by the auction site for selling the item. QXL charges sellers a small listing fee in addition to a percentage of the 'winnings' if the sale goes through. The listing fee is between 15p and £1.25 depending on the cost of the item you have sold. The charge is 5 per cent for the first £15, plus 2.5 per cent of any amount over £15.01 and under £600.01.

Sites to try

Cqout.com – a UK site with the usual product categories but particularly strong on computers and software. Includes charity auctions section where selected charities auction their own merchandise.

eBay.co.uk – the UK branch of the highly popular US site. Huge range of products available but majors in collectables and antiques. Search for products being sold from the UK or get a wider choice from eBay sites in all countries (check that international sellers can ship to UK).

eBid.co.uk – UK site strongest on music and videos, books and magazines, collectables and electrical goods. Auctions for items which have had 5 or more bids are highlighted so you know what the 'hottest' sellers are.

Icollector.com – US site specialising in fine art, antiques and collectables. Buy from dealers and galleries around the world as well as individuals. Lots of high-value items e.g. paintings by famous artists, guitars used by supergroups but lower priced items too.

Loot.com – mainly classified ads but the auction branch of the site is strong on cars and car accessories.

QXL.com – leading site with numerous European branches. Everything from computers to holidays. Clear, easy-to-use site with a good search facility.

Whatamibid.com – UK-based favourite for people buying and selling stamps and coins but many other categories covered.

Auction sites to try

Auction sites can seem complicated to the complete novice. The best way to get acquainted with how auctions work is to browse through a couple of sites. Many sites have auction channels. **Amazon.co.uk**, for example, has its own auction 'wing' dealing in books, music, film and electronics, and the homepage that you get with your ISP is likely to have some sort of auction channel as part of it – Excite and MSN, for example, both have their own auction channels. These are worth a look as an introduction to auction sites, although they may not have the 'traffic' that the leading dedicated auction sites will have.

You can also use one of the specialist online auction directories to link to a variety of sites – try **Auctionwatch.com** or **Bidfind.com** which feature mainly US auction sites but include some UK ones, or look at a general UK shopping directory site such as **Topoftheshops.co.uk** for a more complete list of UK auction sites.

If you visit a web site with the Which? Web Trader logo which includes an auction site, please note that this part of the site is outside the remit of the Web Trader Code of Practice (see Part 3). The law concerning auctions is different to the one applied to normal purchases (everyday transactions) and a consumer's statutory rights can be excluded. It is also likely that your purchase will be from a private individual, not the Which? Web Trader. Which? cannot ensure compliance by these individuals with the code of practice.

Part 2

The Web Directory
– a taste of what's
out there

The Web Directory – a taste of what's out there

Books, CDs and computer software and hardware are the most popular items sold online but you can also buy food, furniture, a holiday, even plants and have them delivered to your door. As the following directory shows, the Internet is a cornucopia.

The web sites included in the following directory have been chosen to illustrate the breadth of choice available to online shoppers. The range changes constantly, and you will find many more leads, especially if you use the shopping directories described elsewhere in the book, but it will get you started and should enable you to find sites for the vast majority of your needs without too great an expenditure of time.

Although we have assessed many of the sites, we have not assessed the merchandise (the range of which changes very rapidly); availability of specific items would in any case be impossible to guarantee. We simply tell you what sort of goods the sites have on offer.

How to use the Directory

We have split the web sites into product categories, such as flowers and cars. Each category in the directory includes a selection of sites ranging from high-street shops to one-man bands. If you know what sort of product you want, look in that category to find a selection of web sites offering that item. We give a brief description of each web site, indicating what it sells and evaluating its layout and ease of use. We also note whether the site is UK-based.

Worth a look gives you an idea of what is special about that site, it may be the bargains, the curiosities on offer or the special deal section.

Delivery gives brief details of the site's delivery charges and time scale. These are estimates based on the delivery information given on each site. (For more on all aspects of delivery, see Chapter 4.)

Many of the sites listed are Which? Web Traders; you can recognise them from the logo in the entry. At the end of most categories we give a round-up of Which? Web Traders. (For a fuller list of Which? Web Traders see Part 3.)

Art and antiques

The Internet provides an ideal medium for making art more accessible to potential buyers who find traditional art galleries exclusive or unwelcoming. Some of the online art sites make a point of stating that they want to bring original art to a wider audience. Small shops selling antiques and collectables have also found a new way of reaching customers via the Internet. It is the auction sites, however, that are a huge attraction for those looking for antiques and collectables. Some auction sites deal only in these – see Chapter 6.

Allegria.co.uk

Online arts and crafts market. Huge range of traditional and contemporary products including pottery, embroidery, collectors' dolls, metalwork, limited edition prints, tableware and ceramics.
WORTH A LOOK: Auction section for potential bargains
DELIVERY: charge varies but is displayed with each product/5-14 days

Antiqueprints.com

Antique maps and prints from established Gloucester-based antique print shop. County maps and town plans included in the map selection. Caricatures and costume designs in the print selection.
WORTH A LOOK: useful links to specialist antique map and print information sites plus general antiques sites
DELIVERY: £1 for one item, included on more than 1 item and on orders over £30 /2–4 days

Artrepublic.com

Contemporary art posters and silk screen prints. Posters feature work by artists from Whistler to Warhol. Search by artist, style or title.
WORTH A LOOK: art terms and artists' biographies sections
DELIVERY: included/3–5 days

Britart.com

Stylish-looking contemporary art site devoted to original works by emerging and established British artists. Buy at the asking price or make an offer and you'll be notified by email within one day if your offer has been accepted.

WORTH A LOOK: 'Art Tab' interest-free credit scheme
DELIVERY: £11.99-£49.99 depending on type of packaging needed/14 days

Easyart.com

Large selection of reproductions, limited edition prints and photographic images. Everything can be mounted and framed by them. Experiment with different frames and mounts on the site to get the look you want.

WORTH A LOOK: 'Artbytes' section for tips on choosing a frame and on hanging the picture
DELIVERY: included/5 days

Inglisantiques.com

Antique ceramics from established Edinburgh antique shop specialising in ceramics circa 1850-1940. Many with a Scottish theme. Condition of the items is made clear on each picture.

WORTH A LOOK: special Royal Doulton section
DELIVERY: included/next day

Londonart.com

More than 200 artists and 2,000 works represented on this online gallery site, including sculpture, installations and photography.

WORTH A LOOK: 'Interiors' section for luxury and unusual *objets d'art* for the home, including carvings from mammoth tusks
DELIVERY: costs and times quoted individually depending on size and type of work

Smartcraft.co.uk

Multitude of craft kits. Choose from needlecraft, appliqué, fabric stencilling, glass and ceramic painting kits, metal craft and parchment craft.

WORTH A LOOK: cross-stitch kits of Disney and Warner Bros favourites including Buzz Lightyear and Scooby-Doo.

DELIVERY: £2.95 under £25, included over £25/21 days

Which? Web Trader round-up

- **Cardinspirations.co.uk** materials for making your own greetings cards
- **Claricecliff.co.uk** Clarice Cliff reproductions by Wedgwood
- **Creationsdirect.co.uk** patchwork and quilting supplies
- **I2w.co.uk** graphic and art materials
- **Lainesworld.co.uk** floral art and craft supplies
- **Pictures-uk.com** posters and prints
- **Studioarts.co.uk** long-established art materials supplier, plus limited-edition prints
- **The-artwork.co.uk** online art gallery specialising in Scottish scenes
- **Tool-signshop.co.uk** hobby tools and craft knives
- **Redrobin.co.uk** paintings, prints, carvings and enamels with a bird and wildlife theme

Books and magazines

This is an area of the Internet where competition is stiff and rife.
For the consumer, this means it's well worth comparing prices
between different sites. Try using one of the price-comparison
search engines to help you do this (see pages 28–30 for suggested
comparison sites to try). You can easily find savings of 35 per
cent on recommended retail prices for current bestsellers. The
biggest and best-known sites may not necessarily be the
cheapest. Try the supermarkets that sell online. Some now sell
bestsellers and price them very competitively.

Alphabetstreet.co.uk

British-run general book site aiming to compete with US giants
such as Amazon and Barnes & Noble. Wide range of titles. Site is
busy-looking but books are easy to find. Big discounts
on their top-ten bestsellers.
WORTH A LOOK: first chapters available to read online
on selected books
DELIVERY: included/2–3 days

Amazon.co.uk

Probably the best-known web site in any category and the most
popular in the UK. Apart from very nearly any book you could
ever want, the site has lots of extra features, including email
recommendations from Amazon's editors, an auction section
and direct links to publishers. Videos, music, software, toys and
gadgets too. Make price comparisons with other sites if you want
to be sure of the cheapest deal.
WORTH A LOOK: you can visit Amazon's French, German, US and
Japanese stores via the site
DELIVERY: £2.16 plus 59p per book/2 days

Antiques-directory.co.uk

The bookstore of this general antiques trade site has 1,500 titles
reflecting all aspects of the antiques world. 70 categories to
explore, covering everything from coins and medals to art deco
ceramics.

Worth a look: the main site for general antiques information plus a Fairs Diary for listings of antique fairs, flea markets and events
Delivery: included/2–4 days

Audiobooks.co.uk

Online branch of 'The Talking Book Shop' in London. Over 6,000 audio books in stock with access to a further 10,000. Classics plus recordings from radio and TV shows. 'Bestsellers' section has 20% off.
Worth a look: listen to selected audio clips online. You can download a free version of software called Real Player to listen to clips
Delivery: £2/2 days

Bol.com

Huge range at this German-owned online bookstore includes access to books in 14 countries, including the USA.
Worth a look: watch TV pictures online of some popular contemporary authors talk about their work
Delivery: £2.95/1–2 days

Bookshop.blackwell.co.uk

Online store of famous Oxford academic book shop. Lots of information on each book plus 'status' category which tells you how long out-of-stock books will take to deliver and if there will be a delay due to reprinting, for example.
Worth a look: link to their student site
Headfiles.com which discounts new and second-hand textbooks
Delivery: included/1–3 days

Clicktso.com

The Stationery Office's web site dedicated to business, professional and official books and documents. The place to come for professional manuals, management yearbooks and Government White Papers. They also offer any title in print in the UK, including bestsellers.
Worth a look: the 'Daily List' section for government publications published that day
Delivery: included/1–3 days

Magazineshop.co.uk

Magazine subscription service. Range of over 650 magazines available from *Vogue* to *Trout and Salmon*. 'Offers' section lists subscriptions available at a discount.

WORTH A LOOK: 'Gift Ideas' lets you specify a subject and provides you with a list of magazine title suggestions

DELIVERY: magazines sent out direct from the publishers so varies with each title

Mapsworldwide.co.uk

Specialists in travel books, maps and atlases. Many items have 20% discount. Everything from A-Zs of UK towns and cities to books on trekking in the Pyrenees and cycling in France. Good selection of route-planning CD-ROMs.

WORTH A LOOK: selection of glossy satellite images of UK and the world

DELIVERY: £1.95 plus 10% of order value before post and packing/3–7 days

Redonionbooks.com

Site dedicated to cookbooks. All the current 'in' titles plus hundreds of less well-known ones. Limited discounts.

WORTH A LOOK: detailed reviews of selected books by people who work in the food trade – for example, baking books are reviewed by a head baker at an Essex family bakery

DELIVERY: included/6 days

Saxons.co.uk

Bargain-basement style store selling surplus books from publishers at low prices. Not the place for recently released titles or current bestsellers but past bestsellers start at 99p each.

WORTH A LOOK: Saxon's book price-comparison feature compares prices at 40 different Internet bookstores

DELIVERY: £1.65 plus 70p per book/1–2 days

Sportsbooksdirect.co.uk

All the books you could want on football, cricket, tennis, rugby or golf at discount prices. Simply designed site that is easy to use.
WORTH A LOOK: interesting 'fan culture' section with books on subjects ranging from footballers' wives to Manchester United in the 1970s
DELIVERY: included/2-5 days

Studentbookworld.com

Discount textbook store. The search engine lists over 1.2 million books. 'Top textbooks' section includes mainstream big sellers too. Price savings clearly displayed.
WORTH A LOOK: have a break from browsing by playing games in the 'Lounge' section
DELIVERY: £2.45-£2.95/2–3 days

Thegoodbookguide.com

Book store with a 'community' feel aimed at serious readers. Readers have significant influence over which books are included and assess and review each title.
WORTH A LOOK: register with the 'Virtual Reading Group' to talk online about a specific book
DELIVERY: £1.95–£2.95/2–4 days

Which? Web Trader round-up

- **Countrybookstore.co.uk** independent online bookstore with over 1 million titles discounted by up to 75%
- **Countryman.co.uk** site specialising in scarce, out-of-print books on horses, dogs, fishing, shooting and various county pursuits
- **Pcbooks.co.uk** specialist computer bookseller
- **Simonlewis.com/bookshop.html** car, motorbike, bus, train and truck books for the enthusiast
- **Schofieldandsims.co.uk** educational schoolbooks, workbooks and dictionaries.

For a full list of Which? Web Traders see Part 3, or go to
www.which.net/webtrader

Cameras and photographic equipment

Cameras available via the Net range from second-hand to the latest digital models. Sites in this category seem evenly divided between those that are offshoots of long-established camera shops or chains and new web-based retailers. Discounts are clearly displayed on most sites. Compare prices if you want the best deal. Try out a couple of price-comparison sites to see what they come up with – **Dealtime.co.uk** and **Kelkoo.com** can both compare prices on selected camera models for you. (For more details on price-comparison sites, see Chapter 2.)

Bestcameras.co.uk

Online store of Kamera Direct, an established mail-order camera supplier. Wide range of brands and types at competitive prices.

WORTH A LOOK: Useful interactive guide to choosing the right camera

DELIVERY: included/1–2 days

Cameracorner.co.uk

Established camera retailer based in Bristol. All kinds of cameras from digital to disposable. Binoculars too. If you are after an item not listed on the site, you can email for availability from the 'bricks and mortar' shop.

WORTH A LOOK: 'Wholesale Warehouse' section for clearance deals

DELIVERY: included/3–5 days

Camerasdirect.co.uk

All types of cameras, many at discount prices.

WORTH A LOOK: 360-degree rotating images available to see on most products

DELIVERY: £4.99/3–5 days

Internetcamerasdirect.co.uk

Web-based retailer selling discount digital cameras and camcorders. Lots of information on each camera but geared towards those with a fair amount of knowledge rather than beginners.

WORTH A LOOK: camera comparison facility to help you choose

DELIVERY: £2.50 under £100, included over/1–5 days

Jessops.com

Online branch of leading photographic retailer. Choice of 20,000 cameras and related products to buy online, including digital and video equipment and darkroom products.

WORTH A LOOK: second-hand equipment section

DELIVERY: £5/2–5 days

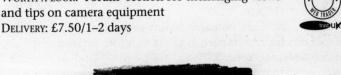

Photographicdirect.co.uk

Digital, video, compact and SLR cameras plus a wide range of lenses, films and accessories. Site is largely geared towards the camera enthusiast and includes a clubs page where you can link to various camera clubs and photographic societies. Camera repair service.

WORTH A LOOK: 'Forum' section for exchanging views and tips on camera equipment

DELIVERY: £7.50/1–2 days

Cars

Car sites represent a significant growth area in Internet selling. Their popularity stems from the fact that they offer easily accessible bargains, cut out the need to visit car showrooms and avoid face-to-face encounters with car salespeople – often an added attraction for many buyers.

The most useful sites will tell you exactly how much you save on the manufacturer's recommended retail price. However, do not expect massive savings on every model. The best savings are more likely to be on top-of-the-range models. Otherwise, savings of a couple of hundred pounds or so are usual.

Check the 'special offers' sections featured on many sites. If you are not particular about buying a specific model, you can get bigger discounts in these sections.

The quoted price on the site generally includes road tax, delivery, registration and any administration fees but check to make sure. Pay any deposit on a credit card for the extra security this gives you.

Autobytel.co.uk

UK branch of leading US car site. Discount new and used cars. Leasing, financing and insurance services, plus you can sell your car through the site.
WORTH A LOOK: 'Car Comparer' facility makes it easy to compare up to 3 cars for aspects such as safety, comfort, exterior and general advantages
DELIVERY: included/7 days to 18 months depending on the car

Caraudiodirect.com

Large range of car stereo and audio equipment at 'best possible' prices.
WORTH A LOOK: chat forum for exchanging views on audio and technical subjects
DELIVERY: included/3 days

Carbusters.com

Internet car-import service developed in conjunction with *Which?* You can save thousands of pounds on new cars imported from Europe. Administration and registration fees required.
WORTH A LOOK: delivery can take time but the 'Instant deals' section highlights cars for which very quick delivery is available
DELIVERY: included/7 days to 11 months depending on the car

Findacarpart.co.uk

Car parts and accessories online shop. Thousands of parts for every vehicle ranging from a single spark to a re-manufactured engine. Part location service for parts not listed on the site.
WORTH A LOOK: free MOT reminding service
DELIVERY: priced by weight plus £1.10 per order/10 days

Fish4cars.co.uk

Second-hand car specialist site owned by a group of regional newspapers. Largest used car database in the country with 180,000 to 200,000 vehicles at any one time. Doesn't sell the cars but acts as 'agent' to dealers private sellers who place the details of their cars on the site.
WORTH A LOOK: 'Fish4Me' service – if you can't find what you want, you can register your desired car details and the ads that match will be emailed to you for a week
DELIVERY: arranged with dealers and private sellers

Importmarques.com

Site specialising in importing top-of-the-range models including Ferrari, BMW, Mercedes, Alfa Romeo and Porsche. All cars are right-hand drive and price includes delivery and VAT.
WORTH A LOOK: personalised Ferrari Source service
DELIVERY: included/delivery time depends on make and model

Jamjar.com

New and used car site owned by Direct Line insurance. Almost all UK cars have 30% off list price. Savings are made clear on the details for each car. Also car rental service and motoring-related products.

WORTH A LOOK: online valuation service if you want to sell your car

DELIVERY: included/14 days to 5 months depending on the car

Speeding.co.uk

Car accessories galore. Fairly basic-looking site but a good place to visit for tyre pressure gauges, speeding radar detectors, security products, car air fresheners and much more.

WORTH A LOOK: 'Special products' section for 'fun' and unusual gadgets including nodding dogs for the back window

DELIVERY: included/3 days

Virgincars.com

This site is clearly designed and easy to use. Choose between custom-built cars or Fast Track new and nearly new cars for speedier delivery. Price includes Virgin Cars Roadside Assistance package (backed by the AA). Savings on manufacturers' retail prices made clear with each model.

WORTH A LOOK: motoring and car-buying advice from a TV motor show presenter, Quentin Wilson

DELIVERY: included/delivery time depends on make and model but for Fast Track cars it is within 6 weeks

Which? Web Trader round-up

- **Autoperfect.net** car valeting products and chemicals
- **Carseekers.co.uk** car import service plus nearly new cars
- **Decibels.co.uk** car audio and security plus navigation and tracking systems
- **Emark.co.uk** car registration numbers
- **TowingBrackets.com** huge listing of towbars

Children's clothing and equipment

The range of childrenswear available online is exceptionally good, and you should be able to find outfits you would not come across in the high street. These sites can make buying for children a pleasurable experience, in sharp contrast to trudging round the shops with them in unhappy tow.

Baby equipment and children's furniture are also worth buying on the Internet – you can easily find standard staples plus more unusual and innovative items. Some of the sites listed below are 'one-stop' sites where you can buy everything you need from pushchairs to pullovers.

Baby-planet.co.uk

Groovy tie-dye baby and toddler clothes. The real-world store is based in Portobello Market in west London. Selection includes tie-dye bibs, bath robes, knotted hats and sleepsuits.
WORTH A LOOK: T-shirts, sweatshirts and cotton jumpers for older children (up to age 6)
DELIVERY: included/3–5 days

Boden.co.uk

'Mini Boden' section has stylish children's clothes for baby to pre-teens. Lots of practical fleecy tops and trousers, plus a more interesting selection of skirts, tops and colourful swimwear. Ordering online is 10% cheaper than buying from the mail-order catalogue.
WORTH A LOOK: original T-shirt designs with images from pirates to fairies
DELIVERY: £3/ 4–6 days.

Charliecrow.com

Site devoted to imaginative dressing-up costumes for ages 18 months to 9 years. Around 70 designs on offer including alien, dinosaur, tiger and princess costumes.

WORTH A LOOK: seasonal fancy dress costumes for Christmas, Halloween or Easter

DELIVERY: included/3–4 days.

Childrenswear.co.uk

Shopping directory site specialising in children's clothes. Links to many well-known high-street store sites including Clarks and Monsoon, 'designer' clothes stores such as Ted Baker, mail-order companies such as Kays and sports shops such as JD Sports.

WORTH A LOOK: classified ads section so you can sell those unwanted pushchairs and toys

DELIVERY: organised via the sites to which you are linked

Cottonmoon.com

All clothes are cotton. Lots of innovative T-shirt designs featuring dinosaurs and other scary creatures. Many of the clothes are sourced from the USA so less likely to see them in UK shops.

WORTH A LOOK: tie-dye section for the modern hippy look

DELIVERY: £3.50/3 days

Debbiebliss.freeserve.co.uk

Knitwear for babies and small children by children's knitwear designer, Debbie Bliss. Choice of ready-made items or kits for knitting yourself. Lots of sea-faring designs from striped jumpers to dresses with nautical motifs.

WORTH A LOOK: free online knitting patterns.

DELIVERY: £4/up to 28 days

Debenhams.com

Casual children's clothes. Wide range including famous brand names as well as Debenhams' own brand.

WORTH A LOOK: selection goes up to age 14 (many other stores stop before this) and style-wise this older range would not embarrass the most cool-conscious early teen.

DELIVERY: £2.95/4–5 days

Gltc.co.uk

The Great Little Trading Company's site is an Aladdin's cave of nursery essentials and safety equipment, home furnishings and travel accessories, plus toys and clothes.

WORTH A LOOK: lots of innovative products you never knew you might need, like the panoramic car rear-view so you can see exactly what the kids are up to in the back

DELIVERY: £3.95/3–5 days

Laredoute.co.uk

Online branch of well-established French mail-order company. Extensive and reasonably priced range of clothes for babies to teens (as well as adult clothes). Good for brands you don't normally find in the UK high street.

WORTH A LOOK: 'best sellers' section for handy inspiration

DELIVERY: £2.45/5–10 days

Mischiefkids.co.uk

Lancashire-based shop selling designer clothing for babies to teens. Browse by designer name. Selection includes DKNY, Moschino, Miniman and Dr Martens. If items are out of stock, this info appears on the site so you don't have to go through the ordering process to find out.

WORTH A LOOK: many items are at the top end of children's clothing in terms of price and the photos of these are worth a browse if only out of curiosity – for example, hand-decorated dresses from Cape Town, South Africa for 0-6 month olds at £52.99

DELIVERY: £2 upwards/3–5 days

Mothercare.com

The leading high-street store for baby and children's clothes and equipment has a wide selection available online. All the practical products you could need, from car seats to baby baths, plus good-value clothing. Not the most imaginative selection but great for essentials and everyday basics.

WORTH A LOOK: a useful special offers section with big savings on selected pushchairs

DELIVERY: £3 under £60, included over £60/7 days

Overthemoon-babywear.co.uk

Specialists in clothes for 0–2 year olds. Tendency towards traditional pastel colours rather than bright designs.
WORTH A LOOK: clothes made from natural fibres only are highlighted – useful for babies with extra-sensitive skin
DELIVERY: included/4 days

Smallfolk.com

Childcare site linked to Great Ormond Street Children's Hospital. Shopping section covers toys, chemist, health, sports, nursery and audio and CDs. Smallfolk gives 5p of every £1 spent to the Great Ormond Street children's charity.
WORTH A LOOK: site is packed with information on childcare, development and health issues
DELIVERY: included/2–10 days

Sundaybest.com

Specialists in christening gowns, dresses and rompers. Everything from shoes and socks to shawls and bibs to match the christening outfit.
WORTH A LOOK: christening gifts section for silverware, pewterware, teddies and books to mark the occasion
DELIVERY: £5/3–5 days

Urchin.co.uk

'Funky' stuff for baby, nursery and small children. Wide range of products, some very practical, some a bit on the wild side, most a talking point. Innovatively designed children's furniture, outdoor wear, bathroom and kitchen products, gifts and toys.
WORTH A LOOK: unusual designer potty range including a spotty potty
DELIVERY: £3.95/2 days

Which? Web Trader round-up

- **Babycare-direct.co.uk** nursery goods specialist
- **Gatefish.com** original children's T-shirts, sweatshirts, fleeces and fancy dress
- **Honfleur.co.uk** christening gowns and accessories
- **Twinkleontheweb.co.uk** washable nappies and other eco-friendly baby products

---

Please let us know of your experiences of shopping online. You can fill in and send us the report form at the end of book or email us at *internetshopping@which.net*

Clothes and fashion

Sports clothes and sturdy outdoor wear have traditionally been the dominant type of clothing available on the Net (perhaps reflecting the fact that most Internet users are male), but since the late 1990s the range of clothes and the sites selling them has blossomed. From designer lingerie to waterproof trousers, the choice and the bargains are out there. The big high-street names such as Marks & Spencer and Debenhams are making their Internet presence known but some of the famous names from whom you would expect to be able to buy online seem hesitant about online sales – at the time of writing, Gap was selling on the Internet in the USA but not in the UK.

Buying clothes online does mean you miss out on the experience of trying clothes on and feeling the material but there has been a long tradition of buying clothes via mail order, and buying online is nothing different. Suffice to say, established mail-order retailers such as Next and Kays see online selling as a simple extension of something they already do very well.

Bloomingmarvellous.co.uk

Non-frumpy maternity clothes. Good selection of casual, formal, sleepwear and underwear. Trousers and skirts have adjustable button elastic so waistband expands with the pregnancy.
WORTH A LOOK: Scholl extra-comfy shoes and boots for tired, pregnancy-laden feet
DELIVERY: £3.95/7 days

Boden.co.uk

Casual own-brand clothes and accessories for men and women from this established mail-order catalogue company. Classically stylish rather than trendy. See also under *Children's clothes and equipment.*
WORTH A LOOK: free trouser tailoring service
DELIVERY: £3/4–6 days

Debenhams.com

Huge choice of clothes for the whole family. Own labels plus well-known brands of sports, casual and designer wear.
Worth a look: special lines designed exclusively for Debenhams by top designers including Jasper Conran and Ben de Lisi
Delivery: £2.95, or included if you spend over £300/4–5 days

Figleaves.com

Underwear for men and women. Famous brands from Aristoc to Charnos to Janet Reger. Mainly 'treat' underwear rather than functional basics.
Worth a look: £5 discount voucher on first order when you register
Delivery: included/1–2 days

Forxl.co.uk

Long trousers for long legs. Site devoted to the clothing needs of tall men, including those with longer than average arms and larger chest sizes. Jeans, chinos, formal trousers and casual shirts.
Worth a look: clearance specials section with up to 50% off
Delivery: included/3 days

Haburi.com

Virtual designer clothes discount factory outlet with 25–50% off normal shop prices. Major names including Calvin Klein, Ghost, Burberry and French Connection. Some sections have limited choice but clothes featured change regularly.
Worth a look: the Haburi club – joining means you get an additional 20% off
Delivery: £2.50 or included if you spend over £70/5 days

IntoFashion.com

Fashion magazine-style site selling clothes with a contemporary feel from established and up-and-coming designers. Many items are sold exclusively by IntoFashion. Designer bags, scarves and other accessories also available.
Worth a look: 50% discount on previous fashion season's stock
Delivery: £2.50/2–5 days

Kiniki.com

Distinctive underwear and swimwear for men. Thongs galore, including the 'Swinger' nylon backless thong and jungle-print designs. More conservative boxers and briefs too.

WORTH A LOOK: 'Misc' section for slinky robes

DELIVERY: £1.50/1–2 days

Landsend.co.uk

'Outdoor' clothing from this US company with a UK base. Think fleeces, Gore-Tex jackets, merino wool jumpers and padded waistcoats. Plus a range of casual and more formal clothes.

WORTH A LOOK: the option to have free fabric swatches sent to you

DELIVERY: £3.50/2 days

Madhouse.co.uk

Online branch of nationwide chain of discount jeans shops. Up to 65% off recommended retail prices. Site has laddish feel to it, aimed at younger man. Well-known brand-name jeans and casual clothes, plus designer labels such as DKNY and Tommy Hilfiger

WORTH A LOOK: clearance section for even bigger discounts on some Levis ranges

DELIVERY: included/5 days

Marksandspencer.com

Extensive range of M&S clothes, shoes and accessories on a stylish and easy-to-use site. Children's clothes available too.

WORTH A LOOK: special sections with clothes for larger and smaller than average sizes

DELIVERY: £2.95/2 days

Next.co.uk

Over 2,000 items from Next stores. Women's, men's and children's clothing including shoes, accessories, underwear and maternity clothes.

WORTH A LOOK: useful and informative size guide section

DELIVERY: £2.50/1 day

Noveltytogs.com

The store to visit for cartoon-character clothes, such as Pokémon T-shirts, Simpsons boxer shorts, South Park slippers, Garfield nightshirts.

WORTH A LOOK: 'Socks' section for the full selection of children's and adult's character socks – everything from Winnie-the-Pooh socks for grown-ups to Spiderman socks for kids

DELIVERY: £1.95/3–10 days

Shoe-shop.com

Huge range from high fashion brands such as Red or Dead through to Clarks and Hush Puppies. Good selection of famous-name trainers too. Search by brand or by specialist categories such as 'wedding shoes' or 'wide fittings'.

WORTH A LOOK: 'factory outlet' section with up to 50% off designer names

DELIVERY: included/3–5 days

Thomaspink.co.uk

Elegant-looking site featuring formal shirts in a variety of cuts and fabrics. 'Matching' service whereby Thomas Pink suggests ties and cufflinks to compliment your chosen shirt. Casual shirts and womenswear also available.

WORTH A LOOK: free gift-wrapping service includes distinctive pink boxes with black ribbon

DELIVERY: £5/3–5 days

Tops.co.uk

Top Shop's 'funky' site clearly aimed at clothes- and cash-conscious teens and twenty-somethings. Clothes are categorised by the look customers are aiming for – 'cute chick', 'city check' or 'spangle', for example. Links to TopMan site.

WORTH A LOOK: 'As featured' section giving highlights of looks from current glossy magazines

DELIVERY: £1.95/next day if order before 3pm

Zercon.com

Designer-name discount clothes with a casual slant. Sweatshirts, polo shirts, jeans, T-shirts and jackets by Calvin Klein, Diesel, Ralph Lauren and Helmut Lang amongst others. Site is functional rather than flash. Men's choice greater than women's.
WORTH A LOOK: competitions to win designer clothes
DELIVERY: £3.50/2–3 days

Which? Web Trader round-up

- **Acorn-printing.co.uk** T-shirts, sweatshirts and caps printed with your own design
- **Beachwear.net** wide range of woman's swimwear
- **Bluebelle.co.uk** sexy adult clothing including PVC, bondage and uniforms ranges
- **Cafecoton.co.uk** stylish French menswear
- **Ecuffs.com** quality cufflinks, shirts and ties
- **Hector-russell.com** kilts and highland dress
- **Pediwear.co.uk** English-made shoes for men including Loake, Padders, Sanders and Alfred Sargent
- **Retrospecs.co.uk** vintage spectacle frames from 1950 to 1980
- **Sizedwell.co.uk** men's and women's outsized casual clothing

Computers and software

Computers and software were amongst the first items to be widely sold on the Internet and the choice available is huge. They are the ideal products for selling on the Internet and as a result there are a large number of sites. This means lots of competition and good prices for consumers.

You can buy direct from the manufacturer (the site address is usually the most obvious – **Apple.com, Dell.co.uk**, **Gateway.com** etc) and these sites tend to let you put together a PC to your requirements. Alternatively, you can buy from a huge choice of dealers. A price-comparison search engine can help you get a better deal (see pages 28–30). It's also worth doing some product research to find out what you need before you buy.

US computer sites have a reputation for offering good deals but make sure you check prices on UK sites and add on delivery charges and any customs duty due before you decide whether or not to buy. (For more detailed information and advice on buying from abroad, see Chapter 5.)

Buy.com

UK branch of major US online computer store. Very wide range of hardware and software including all the big brand names.

WORTH A LOOK: low-price guarantee means the difference is refunded if you find a cheaper product within 24 hours

DELIVERY: included/3–5 days

Cdimports.com

Imported 'back catalogue' CD-ROMs mostly at under £10. Not the place for the latest titles or popular sellers but nevertheless lots of categories covered including games, business, education and lifestyle.

WORTH A LOOK: 'Warehouse Clearance' section for CD-ROMs at £1.99

DELIVERY: 70p per item/5 days

Cortex.co.uk

Computer accessories and products including cartridges, cleaning products, paper, mice and mouse pads, anti-glare screens and diskettes. Selection of software too.

WORTH A LOOK: top ten bestsellers in each category of product to help you choose

DELIVERY: included/3–5 days

Crucial.com/uk

RAM memory manufacturers. Upgrade your computer's memory with their large selection of upgrades for all types of computer.

WORTH A LOOK: selected special prices on bestsellers

DELIVERY: included/1 day

Gamesstreet.co.uk

Large games site selling leading games for PCs, Playstation, Dreamcast, Nintendo 64 and Gameboy at up to 30% off. Educational titles too.

WORTH A LOOK: Streets Online Xchange to buy, sell or exchange games with other private individuals

DELIVERY: included/1–2 days

Learningstore.co.uk

Over 1,000 CD-ROMs based on learning. Revision aids, software to improve sporting or language skills, reference guides, educational games for toddlers and more.

WORTH A LOOK: Budget section for lots of products under £10

DELIVERY: £2.55, or included over £50/2 days

Microwarehouse.co.uk

Another US company that has expanded into the UK. Site has most of the computer equipment you could ever want, including the furniture to put it on. Clear site but it is best if you have an idea of what you want before you visit. Be aware that the most prominent prices displayed do not include VAT.

WORTH A LOOK: 'New Products' section for the latest items on the market

DELIVERY: included/1–2 days

Outpost.com

Popular and well-established US site. Good range and prices (but check UK prices too). Unlike many US sites, this one is geared up for international deliveries.

WORTH A LOOK: gadgets, cameras and gifts too

DELIVERY: charged by weight/3–4 days

Pcworld.co.uk

Online presence of well-known high-street PC superstore. Predictably large selection of hardware and software.

WORTH A LOOK: download section for direct downloading of software

DELIVERY: £3.25/3–5 days

Quietpc.com

Products to 'hush' the noise generated by your PC. Three types of products available geared towards cutting noise from hard drive, power supply or processor cooler.

WORTH A LOOK: lots of good general advice on making your PC quieter

DELIVERY: £6/2–4 days

Softwareparadise.co.uk

Established mail-order software company selling online. Over
100,000 software titles. Search by product, manufacturer's name
or software type. Attractive, easy-to-use site for experienced
buyers and novices alike.

WORTH A LOOK: 'Buyers' Guides' section for useful
'what to look for' advice on a small range of products
DELIVERY: £2.95/2–3 days

Theslammer.com

Games store selling some hardware too. Lots of action games
and a young feel to the site.

WORTH A LOOK: free demo download section
DELIVERY: included/3 days

Which? Web Trader round-up

- **Bigrom.co.uk** discount inkjet cartridges and computer accessories
- **Chipsworld.co.uk** new and second-hand games
- **Consumables.net/** printer and computer online warehouse
- **Justflight.com** flight simulator software specialist
- **Nameyourprice.co.uk** cut-price home office equipment
- **Pcupgrader.co.uk** computer upgrades
- **Unwired.co.uk** hand-held computer specialists
- **Urwired.com** games store

Dating agencies

Online dating is now well-established on the Net. The best-known dating agencies have opened online branches, and introductions via email or agency chat rooms now seem a fairly straightforward and natural way of getting to know a prospective partner in the early stages of a relationship.

Arkline.com

US-based online Jewish introduction agency with an international clientele. Meet secular or orthodox partners. Fees are $30 for 6-month membership, $50 for one year and $130 for three years.

Dateline.co.uk

Probably the best-known UK dating service. Add your own profile straight away for free and browse some profiles of others living near you to get a taste of the service. Cost of membership via the Internet is £99 (£150 normally).

Natural-friends.com

Introduction agency for non-smoking, environmentally concerned singles. Clear site with all the information you need easily accessible. Cost of membership is £20 for 90 days' unlimited access to the profiles on their database plus circulation of your own profile on the site.

DIY

Choice in the DIY sector of online shopping has grown enormously, with big names such as Homebase now selling their vast catalogue of items online, and a good selection of smaller traders offering more specialist products. Many sites offer useful tips and techniques on DIY-related problems, so even if you do not buy, you can use them as a handy reference source.

Bernards.co.uk

Specialist building and architectural ironmongers. Vast selection of 'door furniture' (basically knobs and knockers) plus security products, tools and other general supplies and hardware.
WORTH A LOOK: 'Hot Gossip' online DIY discussion forum
DELIVERY: included for some items, otherwise £4.50/3 days

Focusdoitall.co.uk

Site from the largest independent DIY chain in the UK. Not the full range of products from the stores, but a reasonable selection.
WORTH A LOOK: design ideas section if you need extra inspiration
DELIVERY: £4.99/3 days

Homebase.co.uk

The home and garden subsidiary of Sainsbury's has its entire collection online. Everything from lightbulbs and decorating products to power tools and garden furniture. Clear, easy-to-use site.
WORTH A LOOK: informative and detailed 'Projects' section full of advice on a huge range of DIY jobs
DELIVERY: £4.95/3–4 days

Lockcentre.com

Locks, safes, padlocks, keys and other security products direct to your home. Range includes window locks and digital locks. Discount of 25% off manufacturers' list prices.
WORTH A LOOK: helpline available for DIY installation advice

DELIVERY: price based on weight (automatically calculated during order process)/2 days or 10–14 for safes

---

Screwfix.com

Enormous range of DIY products at wholesale prices. The site even sells washing machine parts. All items are guaranteed to be in stock if they are on the site.

WORTH A LOOK: discount policy means that the more you spend, the greater your discount

DELIVERY: £4.25 on orders under £45, included over/next day

Toolfast.co.uk

Hand- and power-tool specialist. Measuring equipment, workbenches, safety products and a range of other items.

WORTH A LOOK: 'Craft and hobby' section for tools for intricate work such as model-making

DELIVERY: £1.50 under £15, inclusive over/5–8 days

Wallpaperonline.co.uk

Cut-price wallpapers with matching borders and fabrics. 'Paperchaser' search facility lets you specify the room you want to wallpaper and choose the type of design, texture and colour of paper you want then it comes up with suggestions.

WORTH A LOOK: tips and advice on hanging wallpaper, useful for beginners

DELIVERY: included/4–7 days

Which? Web Trader round-up

- **Discountedheating.co.uk** all sorts of heating and plumbing materials and equipment
- **Getools.co.uk** tools for the modern workshop
- **Kitchen-sinks.co.uk** everything to do with and including the kitchen sink
- **Plumbworld.co.uk** taps, showers and plumbing equipment
- **Robertdyasdirect.co.uk** site of the well-known hardware chain

Electrical goods

The full range of electrical products is available online from fridge-freezers to hi-fi equipment. Some sites are better than others at providing useful, balanced product-buying information. Compare prices too – sites that make loud claims for cheap prices may not necessarily be the cheapest.

Applianceonline.co.uk

Leading-name domestic appliances with up to 20% off typical high-street prices. Bosch, Neff, Smeg and others.
WORTH A LOOK: 'American Style' section for distinctive US-made large fridge-freezers and washing machines
DELIVERY: included/2 days –3 weeks depending on make and product

Beststuff.co.uk

Idea behind this site is that they stock only what they judge to be the best product within a specific category, i.e. they stock only one upright vacuum cleaner (Dyson), one DVD player (Toshiba), one digital camcorder (Samsung) and so on. Good explanations on why they have chosen specific products.
WORTH A LOOK: the choice at other sites and shops can sometimes feel overwhelming so simply looking at the small product range on this site could help you make a decision
DELIVERY: included/4–7 days

Comet.co.uk

Online branch of the high-street electrical chain. Over 2,000 products available from small electrical appliances to hi-fis and washing machines. Claim to have the widest range of electrical products to buy online.
WORTH A LOOK: 'Comet favourites' section for highlighted goods that change weekly – often included because they have performed well in independent specialist magazine tests
DELIVERY: £3.99–£21.99 depending on type of product/ timing depends on stock availability and product

Cookers-direct.co.uk

Family-run concern selling wide range of leading-name cookers.
Electric, gas or dual fuel. Free-standing and built-in
models.

WORTH A LOOK: links to all their manufacturers' web
sites – useful for extra information on specific cookers
DELIVERY: included/5–21 days

Letsautomate.com

Home automation store. Gadgets to control opening and closing
your curtains and blinds, lights, heating, garage doors and to let
you watch a video in a different room to where your video
recorder is. Plus home security and telephone automation
systems, touchscreen remote controls and video-camera kits.

WORTH A LOOK: unusual items include a 'sound transducer' that
adds a cinematic 'sensaround' effect when you are
watching videos – it literally shakes the floor under
your seat when you are watching explosive moments!
DELIVERY: £3.53 or included over £100/1–2 days

Richersounds.co.uk

Hi-fi specialist selling 'separates' (individual components you
pick and choose to build your own ideal system) rather than 'all-
in-one' systems. They promise to beat the price on any other
web site by £50.

WORTH A LOOK: useful 'beginner's guide' to buying a
hi-fi system
DELIVERY: £8 for first hi-fi item, £5 for subsequent
ones on the same order/5 days

Simplyradios.com

All the main radio brands, including the full range of
classic Roberts Radios in every colour and style.

WORTH A LOOK: selection of radios for those with
special needs
DELIVERY: included/10 days

Tesco.com

Not content to just sell groceries, Tesco now has an electrical online shop. Over 1,200 products including washing machines, vacuum cleaners, DVDs, phones and cookers.

WORTH A LOOK: 'Price Check' box on each product page shows the comparative price of the product at Comet, Dixons and Argos

DELIVERY: included/3–16 days

Vacuumcleanersdirect.com

Over 250 models from leading brands at discount prices. Selection includes specialist cleaners for pet owners or for those suffering from allergies. Carpet and steam-cleaners, floor polishers. light-weight cleaners and ex-display models available.

WORTH A LOOK: 'Kids corner' for Electrolux and Dyson mini-versions for children

DELIVERY: included/7 days

Value-direct.co.uk

Discount domestic appliances and electricals. Clear and practical site with four ways to search for a product: by model number, by brand/price, by feature or by browsing the stock. Lots of information on the different types of products, plus explanations of technical jargon.

WORTH A LOOK: useful product comparison feature which enables you to compare the features of different models of the same product, presenting the data in an easy-to-read chart format

DELIVERY: included/5–21 days

Webelectricals.co.uk

Good selection of the latest TVs, DVDs, VCRs, hi-fis, camcorders and personal organisers at discount prices. Informative 'buyers' guides' and product info.

WORTH A LOOK: 'Award Winners' section for products they have judged to be the best in specific categories based on performance, build and value for money

DELIVERY: included/1–10 days

Whitebox.co.uk

Washing machine, dishwasher and dryer specialist with a strong consumer-friendly streak. Placing emphasis on unbiased buying advice, *Which?* and *Good Housekeeping* buying guide results are provided, with info on where you can get a product cheaper elsewhere.

WORTH A LOOK: chart-form comparisons of different brands and models make it easy to compare products on the basis of aspects such as energy rating and spin speed

DELIVERY: included/2–10 days

Which? Web Trader round-up

- **Digitalchoice.co.uk** 'state-of-the-art' electrical products
- **Electricsavers.co.uk** small electrical appliance specialists, e.g. shavers
- **Electrical.coop.co.uk** Co-op's electrical e-store
- **Hifibitz.co.uk** all your hi-fi needs
- **Optimair.co.uk** air-conditioning products
- **Teletronics.co.uk** discount electrical retailer
- **Toade.com** car audio and security specialist

It can often be useful to be armed with background information on the type of product you want before you 'go shopping'. The specialist information sites listed in Part 4 can help you.

Financial services

Most of the big banks and building societies have web sites selling the range of services, and sometimes more, that they offer in the high street. Online banking is popular with the banks themselves because in the long run it is cheaper for them as overheads are lower (whether or not these savings are always passed on to the customer is another matter). However, consumers have been slow to take up these services and products – only 0.2 per cent of the UK population currently 'e-bank'.

Unless you know you want to deal with a specific company, the most useful sites for making sure you are spending your money wisely are those that offer comparative information on different companies' financial products. The traditional high-street banks and building societies are not the only companies offering online financial services and you may prefer to deal with other less well-known companies. The sites offering comparative information can help you do this. You can shop around for the best mortgage or insurance deal just by visiting one site. (See Part 4 for details of informative financial web sites.)

Banking/savings

For a complete list of online banking web sites see the British Bankers Association's web site at **www.bankfacts.org**

Co-operativebank.co.uk

The first bank to set up free online banking. This site offers all the usual range of banking services. The Co-op is also behind the Internet-only bank **www.smile.co.uk**, aimed at younger customers.

WORTH A LOOK: section on ethical and ecological banking

Always remember the two basic rules of investing:

- Invest only what you can afford to lose.
- If it sounds too good to be true, then it probably is.

Egg.co.uk

Internet arm of the Prudential. Offers competitive rates on Internet-only savings accounts. You can manage your savings and apply for loans. Also mortgage, insurance and investment products.

WORTH A LOOK: use the shopping section to get money off products using your Egg credit card

Natwest.com

Site offering the usual online banking facilities such as checking your balance and paying bills. It also boasts an online share-dealing service plus useful general information covering e.g. small businesses, students and buying a home or a new car. Fairly typical representative of the kind of thing offered by most high-street bank's online branches.

WORTH A LOOK: one of the increasing numbers of banks now offering WAP (Internet mobile phone) banking services

Insurance

1stquote.co.uk

Insure almost anything you want, including pets and motor breakdowns. Lots of helpful information including an insurance glossary and a 'buyer's guide' to insurance.

WORTH A LOOK: 'talk' live to an online insurance operator via your keyboard or use your PC's microphone and speakers

Directline.com

Car, home, travel and life insurance to buy online. Apply online for a loan too.

WORTH A LOOK: 'Special offers' section for various cheaper deals

Eaglestardirect.co.uk

Car, home, travel, life and boat insurance available online. Clear site with straightforward information.

WORTH A LOOK: pose any question about insurance to Catherine, Eagle Star's virtual agent

Easycover.com

Car, home or travel insurance. Fill in an online form and you receive quotes from a range of insurers by email or instantly online.

WORTH A LOOK: quote service for life, pet, health, motorcycle, boat and caravan insurance due to be added to site

Screentrade.co.uk

Internet insurance 'supermarket'. Use the comparison facility to compare quotes from different insurance companies. You type in what you want and a table with comparative details comes up. You then choose a policy and buy online.

WORTH A LOOK: the price pledge means that if you find a cheaper quote elsewhere, the difference will be refunded

Mortgages

Alliance-leicester.co.uk

Mortgages online from this leading lender. All the information you need is there but perhaps a bit too business-like in tone and appearance.

WORTH A LOOK: 'Budget Planner' facility which lets you type in all your monthly outgoings and income to help you see what you can afford

Charcolonline.co.uk

Mortgage comparison site that is part of a large independent financial advice company. Access to more than 500 mortgages from over 45 different lenders. Includes products exclusive to Charcol. Mortgage deals from high-street lenders plus more specialist companies.

WORTH A LOOK: 'best-buy' summary charts showing recommended deals for fixed rate, discount rate and capped mortgages

Moneygator.com

Attractive-looking site that enables you to compare a range of mortgages available from different companies via the site. Fill in one form and you can apply to multiple banks and building societies at the same time. Detailed information on how to choose a mortgage and understand how they differ. Use the site to find credit card and personal loan deals too.

WORTH A LOOK: useful calculators to work out how much you can borrow and what your monthly costs will be

Pensions

Ins-site.co.uk

Compare pension and life insurance products using one site. Ins-site has a 'panel' of leading providers – you access their products using Ins-site's comparison summaries to compare charges and long-term investment results.

WORTH A LOOK: useful information on different types of pension provision plus handy glossary of life insurance and pensions terms

Legalandgeneral.co.uk

Many companies selling pensions now make it easy for you to apply online. Look at the Legal and General site to see how it's commonly done. The EPension scheme lets you fill in an application form with all the necessary details online. You then need to print it off and send it to the company (other sites let you send the form online but will send you back a printed copy in the post so that you can sign it).

WORTH A LOOK: Pension Quick Guide for lots of useful info

Shares

Barclays-stockbrokers.co.uk

Good for beginners – the Online Share Dealing Guide takes you through the share-dealing process. Online dealing demos are useful too. Barclays charge 1% commission with a minimum of £11.99 and a maximum of £39.99.

WORTH A LOOK: 'Terminology Explained' section for useful jargon-busting

Etrade.co.uk

Popular US share-dealing site now in the UK. The basic commission is £14.50 for deals under £1,500, or £19.50 if over this.

WORTH A LOOK: 'Test Drive' section for beginners – you can simulate your first online trade in six easy steps

Sharexpress.co.uk

The share-dealing arm of the Halifax. Buy or sell shares over the Internet and manage your share portfolio from your PC. Good site for beginners with easy-to-use design. Commission is from £12.50 to £50 depending on the value of the deal.

WORTH A LOOK: occasional special offers on their commission charges

Sharepeople.com

Independent online stockbroker 'bringing shares and people together'. Extensive amount of information but more accessible for those with some experience rather than the complete novice. Charges from £5 per trade.

WORTH A LOOK: 'Sharepeople Education Centre' for details on online training courses in investing, plus discount books on share dealing

Which? Web Trader round-up

- **Abgltd.co.uk** insurance broker and independent financial advisor
- **Direct-travel.co.uk** travel insurance specialist
- **Fredfindsmortgages.com** seeks out good mortgage deals
- **Gfm-ifa.co.uk** independent financial advisors
- **Policydirect.co.uk** Internet-only insurance company
- **Rapidinsure.co.uk** wide range of insurance policies offered
- **Studentwatchout.co.uk** insurance for students and young professionals
- **Wisemoney.com** instant quotes for a range of financial services from different companies

Flowers

There appears to be very little difference between online flower-ordering sites. All the sites seem to offer a similar service; some are more sophisticated. Delivery costs tend to be included in the price but remember to check for extras such as service charges. For next-day delivery, you usually have to order before a certain time of day. Check on this.

Crocus.co.uk

Flowers and flowering houseplants. Go to the 'cut flowers' section of this general gardening shopping site for a simple selection. Mixed bouquets at three different prices, bunches of lilies and roses and a range of houseplants including orchids and jasmine.

WORTH A LOOK: the information on the flowers is good – the site tells you what you get for your money (e.g. the number of roses in a small bunch) and gives advice on how to look after the houseplants

DELIVERY: included/next day for flowers, up to a week for houseplants

Flowersdirect.co.uk

All flowers imported from Dutch growers. Wide choice including elaborate basket arrangements and more unusual items such as orchids growing on tree bark.

WORTH A LOOK: 'Minimalist' selection for simple, contemporary designs

DELIVERY: included/next day

Freesia.co.uk

Specialist in Lincolnshire-grown scented freesias. Mixed colour, single colour or combination bouquets.

WORTH A LOOK: advice on choosing and looking after freesias as well as growing your own

DELIVERY: included/next day

Interflora.co.uk

Key in your flower, colour and price, or choose from 'customer favourites' section or the full catalogue.

WORTH A LOOK: free reminder service – you put important dates and information into your Interflora address book and site reminds you

DELIVERY: included (although £3.20 service charge)/ next day

Marksandspencer.com

M&S offer some attractive bouquets on this site – take a look at the colourful 'Tropical Paradise' bouquet or stylish single orchid plant. Delivery charge quite high compared to some other sites.

WORTH A LOOK: add chocolates, a teddy, champagne or a vase to your order

DELIVERY: £4/next day

Which? Web Trader round-up

All the following offer a similar service, including next-day delivery:

- **Clareflorist.com**
- **Firstflowers.com**
- **Flowergram.co.uk**
- **Flowers2send.com**

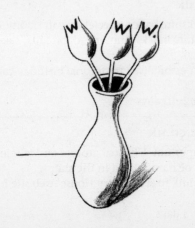

Food

A good range of shops now sell food online. Supermarket food is what many people want – Tesco and Iceland have led the way in this area and other supermarkets are catching up.

Sites selling specialist foods are common and you can order anything from laverbread to cheeses from one-man-band cheese-makers. Delivery costs tend to be quite high because of the need for packaging that protects the food during transit.

8oohampers.com

Scottish food hampers from £17.99 to £89.99. Hampers for special occasions from Mother's Day to Christmas.
WORTH A LOOK: whisky lovers' hampers
DELIVERY: £5.95/3 days

Bluemango.co.uk

Condiment store. Chutneys, jams, honeys, salsas, mustards and sauces. Lots of unusual flavours such as roman nut mustard.
WORTH A LOOK: range of gift boxes includes hot sauce selection
DELIVERY: £4/3–5 days

Botham.co.uk

Family-run Yorkshire bakers specialising in traditional Yorkshire produce. Yorkshire brack, plum bread, biscuits, cakes and preserves.
WORTH A LOOK: personalised traditional birthday-cake service
DELIVERY: £4.75/2–10 days

Chilli-willie.co.uk

Curry spice emporium. Unusual ground and whole spices that can be hard to find in the shops.
WORTH A LOOK: link to 'The Curry House' web site for curry recipes
DELIVERY: £2.99/3 days

Cybercandy.co.uk

Sweets from around the world. Hershey bars and Babe Ruths from the USA, 'cream salty candy' from China, plus sweets from Japan, Australia, New Zealand and Taiwan.

WORTH A LOOK: regular competitions to win free sweets and T-shirts

DELIVERY: £1.74/3–5 days

Iceland.freeshop.com

The frozen-food chain delivers fresh and grocery products as well as frozen. No genetically modified ingredients in its own-label products.

WORTH A LOOK: clear symbol system if you want to watch out for certain aspects of products including microwaveable, vegetarian and organic

DELIVERY: included but orders have to be over £40/next day if ordered before 3pm

Leapingsalmon.co.uk

Gourmet 'meal kits' delivered to your home. They provide all the ingredients, including the vegetables, sauces and accompaniments, ready to cook. All you have to do is follow their recipe. Recipes change regularly – main course examples include 'Swordfish in banana leaves' (£18.50 for 2) or 'Pollo Limone' (£17.50 for 2). Three-course set menus are also available e.g. grilled vegetables/roasted duck in port/chocolate mousse (£32.90 for 2).

WORTH A LOOK: 'Splash' loyalty scheme to build up points to qualify for a free meal

DELIVERY: £4.50/next day (same day in central London)

Organicsdirect.co.uk

Organic fruit and vegetables delivered by the box from small organic farmers and growers. Organic dairy produce, baby food, wine, bread and other groceries too.

WORTH A LOOK: 5% discount on each order if you set up a regular order

DELIVERY: included if vegetable box is part of order/2–5 days

Teddingtoncheese.co.uk

Online branch of established cheese shop selling huge range of British and continental cheeses. Traditional types plus newer, unusual cheeses made by small producers.

WORTH A LOOK: themed cheese boards including 'The Picnic' and 'The Robert' (Scottish cheeses)

DELIVERY: £5.95/2 days

Tesco.com

The most established online supermarket delivery service. All the supermarket food you could need. Wide range of organic produce included in the range.

WORTH A LOOK: 'Express Shopper' facility speeds up your food search – you list the things you want and the Express Shopper automatically finds them for you

DELIVERY: £5/you choose a suitable time slot – usually 1–3 days

Thefishsociety.co.uk

UK's biggest online fishmonger. Around 150 varieties of quality frozen fish available. Specialists in more unusual fish.

WORTH A LOOK: interesting non-fish products include samphire and laverbread

DELIVERY: £10 orders up to £50, £5 over £50/1–4 weeks

Welshlambdirect.co.uk

Welsh lamb from group of local farmers in Dyfi Valley, west Wales. Bulk buy 'Traditional' or 'Quick Lamb' packs with range of cuts. 'Half' or 'Full' lamb sizes at £35–£70.

WORTH A LOOK: free recipe brochure can be sent to you on request

DELIVERY: £3–£5/10 days

Whittard.com

Over 150 types of speciality tea and over 20 fresh coffees direct from the high-street tea company.

WORTH A LOOK: special section on how to brew the perfect cup of tea or coffee

DELIVERY: £2.95, or included over £30/2–3 days

Which? Web Trader round-up

- **Brownes.co.uk** handmade chocolates
- **Coffee-tree.co.uk** arabica bean coffee roasted in France
- **Colestrad.co.uk** Christmas puddings, clootie dumplings. Fruit cakes and other traditional English puddings
- **Eshopone.co.uk** look at this general site to find Roney's High Class Butchers selling Orkney Island beef, rare breeds pork and more
- **Gourmet2000.co.uk** French-style deli foods
- **Iorganic.co.uk** organic fruit and veg
- **Martins-seafresh.co.uk** Internet branch of fishmongers in Cornwall
- **Mckean.co.uk** traditional Scottish meat products including haggis
- **Mountfuji.co.uk** Japanese foods
- **Olives.uk.com** gourmet olives plus Mediterranean fare

You can find out whether a supermarket delivers to your area by checking its web site. At the time of writing Asda, Iceland, Sainsbury's and Tesco offer web-based grocery shopping with home delivery.
For the results of a *Which?* user trial, see 'Meals on Wheels', *Which?*, March 2001.

Garden

Gardening sites are plentiful on the Net. Many of them boast a huge range of plants and equipment, plus good advice sections on a multitude of gardening issues. Some sites are useful sources for gift ideas, offering decorative and unusual gardening paraphernalia as well as more standard gardening products.

Crocus.co.uk

Large, stylish-looking gardening site. Choice of over 8,000 plants, tools and gardening gifts. Cut flowers and Christmas tree service too.

WORTH A LOOK: 'Plant Doctor' service – email an expert with a gardening problem and you'll receive a response within 48 hours

DELIVERY: £3.95 upwards depending on cost of order/3–15 days

Dig-it.co.uk

Gardening site with good selection of bulbs, plants, garden furniture, tools and equipment.

WORTH A LOOK: 'Limited Edition' section for the style-conscious gardener featuring unusual garden sculptures (for example, 'Mating Ducks')

DELIVERY: £3.95/7–10 days

Gardening365.com

Plants, seeds and all sorts of gardening equipment and miscellaneous items supplied by a wide range of gardening retailers via this site. Useful for more unusual plants and gardening items such as Giant Sequoia tree seedlings and bees' nests.

WORTH A LOOK: 'Find-a-Gardener' advertising service

DELIVERY: charge varies and is automatically calculated on order/7 days

Gardenbuildingsdirect.co.uk

Range of garden sheds, greenhouses, summerhouses, log cabins and children's playhouses.

WORTH A LOOK: useful links to gardening advice sites and manufacturers' sites

DELIVERY: included/17 days

Greenfingers.com

Busy-looking site selling most things you could want for a garden, plus lots of gardening news and advice.

WORTH A LOOK: 'Ask George' gardening reference service providing a range of information including specialist nursery search facility

DELIVERY: £2.95/15 days

Grogro.com

Online garden shop backed by the Royal Horticultural Society. As well as RHS books, gifts and tickets for events, you can buy a wide range of plants and gardening products.

WORTH A LOOK: join the Royal Horticultural Society online with benefits including free entry to RHS gardens and flower shows

DELIVERY: included for many items, heavier items charged by weight/times vary depending on product

Hammocks.co.uk

Relax in the garden in a handwoven Mexican hammock or hammock chair. The Mexican Hammock Company, which runs the site, buys from co-operative-based groups in rural Mexico.

WORTH A LOOK: site also sells handmade mirrors, tiles, blankets and pottery

DELIVERY: £5/7 days

Mowerworld.co.uk

Big selection of electric and petrol mowers, trimmers and hedgecutters from this online version of established Nottingham-based mower retail specialist. All the main names in mowers available.

WORTH A LOOK: 'Lawn Care Tips' section full of useful advice on looking after a lawn

DELIVERY: £3.95/2 days

Roses.co.uk

Specialist rose site from Harkness, an established family-run firm of rose growers. Useful 'Rose Selector' feature where you select the colour, type and even scent of the rose you are after and the site comes up with suggestions.

WORTH A LOOK: 'Getting the best from your roses' section for planting and care advice

DELIVERY: £2.95/time varies because of the seasonal nature of the product – orders are collected throughout the year and bare-root roses despatched late October–early March

Shrubsdirect.com

Over 1,000 varieties of garden-centre size plants from a wholesale nursery in Cheshire. It claims that because it sells wholesale its prices are cheaper than at local garden centres. Minimum order of 6 plants.

WORTH A LOOK: 'Big Spenders' section for trees

DELIVERY: £2–£4/2 days

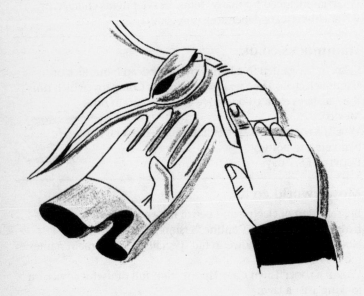

Which? Web Trader round-up

- **Cmsgardens.co.uk** family-run greenhouse and garden specialist
- **E-garden.co.uk** general gardening site
- **Equatics.co.uk** aquatic accessories at discount prices
- **Mowers-online.co.uk** discount mowers and garden machinery
- **Nickys-nursery.co.uk** flower seed specialist – range includes herb and wild flower seeds
- **Poolstore.co.uk** swimming pool products including chemicals and floating loungers
- **Solosite.net/pyromid** outdoor cooking equipment
- Thetinpot.co.uk: garden equipment and gifts for indoor and outdoor gardeners

For a review of some gardening sites, see *Gardening Which?*, August 2000.

Gifts

The Internet is great for discovering interesting and unusual items you do not come across in the ordinary high street. For those who dread trudging round the shops for birthdays or Christmas presents, the Net can seem like a dream come true. However, if you like putting a reasonable degree of thought into present-buying, you can find yourself spending ages trawling the sites for 'that special something' – the choice can sometimes be overwhelming. The Internet seems particularly flushed with sites selling gismos and gadgets.

Lots of the sites selling gift-type items will have a gift-finder facility to help you with suggestions – you type in the interests and hobbies of the person for whom you are buying the present and the site comes up with results. Many sites offer a gift-wrapping service.

It is worth looking at the other sections of the Directory for gift ideas – keen gardeners, sports fanatics, DIY and car buffs, fashion and jewellery fans and bookworms are all catered for in the appropriate categories. The 'Flowers' section on pages 122–3 should help with Mother's Day and Valentine's gifts too.

Aardvarkstore.com

Specialist cigar site selling over 300 types of cigar from Cuba, Nicaragua, Dominican Republic, Honduras and others. Cigar samplers available with different types in one small selection.

WORTH A LOOK: selection of cigar accessories including humidors (specially made cigar boxes) and cutters

DELIVERY: £6, included for samplers/3–7 days

Adventureshop.co.uk

Gift vouchers for flying and driving adventures, including hot-air balloon flights, flying in a fast jet or driving a rally car.

WORTH A LOOK: 'Adventure' gadgets too such as a 'wrist top' computer and an electronic hand-held moving map

DELIVERY: included/2–3 days

Alt-gifts.com

Wide range of out-of-the-ordinary gifts. Shop within categories such as 'What's hip', 'Action Lady', 'The Love section' and 'Novelty jewellery'. Lots of gadgets plus departments for kids and home.

WORTH A LOOK: 'Ask the expert' gift service – you type in the interests of the person you are buying for and it comes up with suggestions

DELIVERY: £1.79 plus 50p per item/5–10 days

Asseenonscreen.com

Buy what you see on film and TV. Desirable objects from films and TV shows – not the original but similar. Examples include chair as seen in *Big Brother* and distinctive cups and saucers as featured in the café scenes in *Friends*.

WORTH A LOOK: 'New products' section for the latest additions to the site

DELIVERY: £2.95 for orders under £50, included over/5 days

Bbcshop.com

A wealth of BBC products including spin-off books and videos from popular TV programmes such as *Walking with Dinosaurs*. Also Tweenies toys, BBC radio audio cassettes and CDs plus BBC language courses packs.

WORTH A LOOK: Children's section for all the fans of Noddy, Fireman Sam, Scooby-Doo, Tom & Jerry, Pingu, Teletubbies etc.

DELIVERY: £1.95–£2.95 for up to 4 products, included over/2–3 days

BestofBritish.com

Sounds like a tourist-targeted site selling shortbread and plastic London buses but is actually a very stylish site full of classic and modern British-designed goods. Selection includes Mulberry accessories, Aquascutum luggage, Brora cashmere, Jasper Conran T-shirts, Cath Kidson floral bedlinen and Molton Brown cosmetics. Delivery deadline, however, seems unnecessarily long.

WORTH A LOOK: 'New designers' section for the latest looks and accessories

DELIVERY: £2.95, included over £100/21 days

Chocolatestore.com

Gourmet truffles, pralines and liqueurs, mostly handmade. Also traditional English violet and rose creams. 'Luxury Chocolate Feast' hamper contains a variety of chocolate treats from 'Grand Cru' chocolate pearls to Pure Drinking Chocolate Flakes.
WORTH A LOOK: site is part of **Allpresent.com** which sells flowers, drinks, cakes and cards too.
DELIVERY: £2.40/3–5 days

Crueltyfreeshop.com

Animal-friendly online store with a range of gift ideas including unbleached cotton or animal-rights slogan T-shirts, vegan chocolates and non-animal-tested cosmetics and toiletries.
WORTH A LOOK: charity donations section makes it easy for you to donate online to a range of animal charities
DELIVERY: price depends on weight/14 days

Firebox.com

Latest gadgets and grown-up toys including watch cameras, high-tech spinning top, everlasting 'blue' light torch, plus classics such as Swiss army knives.
WORTH A LOOK: top five gadgets list
DELIVERY: £1.95–£3.95/1–3 days

Frasersautographs.com

Original autographs and signatures of famous people. Choose by name or by category – for example, British politicians, artists, pop stars. Autographs from historic and current figures. A division of Stanley Gibbons.
WORTH A LOOK: auction section for details of online autograph auctions
DELIVERY: £6/2–3 days

Kitsch.co.uk

A site devoted to kitsch and retro-style goodies. Lava lamps, Japanese robot toys, chilli lights, plus 'one-offs' such as the Wonder Woman address book or the Elvis pendulum clock.

WORTH A LOOK: 'Kitsch History' section for all you need to know about this area of popular culture
DELIVERY: price depends on weight/7 days

Liberty.co.uk

Online branch of the stylish, long-established London department store. Fashion accessories, home furnishings and other gift ideas available.
WORTH A LOOK: 'Limited Edition' section for art nouveau-style clocks, ornaments and tea sets from original Liberty designs
DELIVERY: £5/7 days

Moma.org

US site. New York's Museum of Modern Art's online store is a good place for gifts you won't see in UK shops. Stylish designer furniture and accessories for the home plus kids' and fashion items. Useful gift ideas section.
WORTH A LOOK: if you can't afford the original designer chairs on the site, there are collectable mini-versions too
DELIVERY: price depends on weight/delivery time depends on product and shipping method chosen

Nottingham-lace.co.uk

Tablecloths, shawls, bedspreads, lingerie, handkerchief sets and more all in lace.
WORTH A LOOK: 'made to measure' service
DELIVERY: £2.75 or 15% of net price, whichever is highest/7–9 days

OutofAfrika.co.uk

African design with a strong contemporary edge. Not the place for tourist-targeted elephant carvings. Instead, an interesting and unusual selection including ostrich egg bowls, cow-skin cushions and carpets, leather-topped tables, hand-beaded silverware and

dried and decorated Monkey Balls (a fruit a bit like a pomegranate).
WORTH A LOOK: 'Personal Gifts' section for original ideas including hand-painted children's china, an African poker game and boxed greetings cards
DELIVERY: £3.50, included over £150/3–5 days

Pushposters.com

Vast collection of music posters – just the thing for a teenager's bedroom walls. Search for posters by artist. List of top 30 most requested artists to help you choose.
WORTH A LOOK: music calendars, clothing and tour books
DELIVERY: £2.50–£3.50 or included on orders over £100/21 days

Remember-when.co.uk

Archive newspaper collection. Copies of original newspapers from 1642 to date. Show a friend/relative what was headline news on the day he or she was born.
WORTH A LOOK: perpetual calendar lets you type in a birth date and it tells you what day of the week that was
DELIVERY: included/2 days

Thingstoengrave.co.uk

Engraved gifts online. Silverware including photo frames, tankards, small mirrors, christening cups. Engraving is £4 per item.
WORTH A LOOK: browse the gift categories for ideas – 'For him', 'For her', 'Retirement', 'Wedding', 'Anniversary'
DELIVERY: included/3–5 days

Vandashop.co.uk

Victoria & Albert Museum's shop site sells an eclectic range of tasteful and unusual gifts. Home furnishings, ceramics, pictures and prints, books, jewellery and cards.
WORTH A LOOK: 'Gift finder' facility lets you choose the age and sex of the person you are buying for as well as the cost of the gift
DELIVERY: £5.95–£7.50/5 days

Which? Web Trader round-up

- **Aanside.co.uk** stained glass and carved wooden gifts from the A'anside craft studios in the Scottish highlands
- **Allthingscornish.com** everything from clotted cream to Cornish art
- **Businesstoys.co.uk** solve executive stress with a fur PC cover
- **Chess-shops.com** unusual chess sets and pieces
- **Chiasmus.co.uk** 'fresh and funky' products for the home
- **Partydomain.co.uk** party accessories galore
- **Penhome.co.uk** specialists in vintage fountain pens
- **Psi-soft.co.uk** collectable cards including Pokémon and Digimon
- **Thecardstore.co.uk** buy your cards online

Health and beauty

This range includes general sites selling everything from over-the-counter medicines and lipsticks to pills for pets. You can also organise prescription deliveries online and get email advice from pharmacists.

Ainsworths.com

Well-known manufacturer and supplier of homeopathic remedies now selling online. Site aimed at professional homeopaths and interested amateurs, although information for those new to homeopathy is limited. Massive range of remedies to cover every ailment.

WORTH A LOOK: online magazine for the latest in homeopathic news and research

DELIVERY: £2 for 1–10 items, by weight for heavier parcels/3–5 days

Bigboycondoms.co.uk

Online condom store. Save up to 40% on Durex, Mates and Safex brands.

WORTH A LOOK: musical section for condoms that play tunes including 'Love me Tender' and 'Happy Birthday'

DELIVERY: included/2–3 days

Blademail.co.uk

Site devoted to razor blades and shaving products. Gillette, Phillips and Wilkinson Sword brands. Ladies shaving selection too.

WORTH A LOOK: register with the regular automatic delivery service and blades will always be delivered before you run out

DELIVERY: price is based on weight so varies but 39p for a pack of blades/2–4 days

Blushingbuyer.co.uk

Products and info for people suffering from embarrassing personal problems such as acne, bad breath, haemorrhoids and smelly feet. Plus contraceptive and sensual products such as massage oils.

WORTH A LOOK: read 'Blusher of the month' feature for embarrassing tales

DELIVERY: included/1–5 days

Changeslive.com

Uncluttered beauty site with decent range of leading brand make-up and beauty products. Special section for men containing men's fragrances, moisturisers, 'grooming' kits and more.

WORTH A LOOK: Changeslive beauty studio – get an online makeover by viewing different styles on a photograph of yourself (you need to upload a digital photo)

DELIVERY: £2.95, included over £10/2 days

Fragrancedirect.co.uk

Cut-price perfume store with many designer brands. Majority of products are store-counter testers so no fancy packaging, hence lower prices.

WORTH A LOOK: gift-wrapping service at £1.25 if you want more than the basic bottle

DELIVERY: £1 per bottle/5 days

Lookfantasic.com

Salon-brand hair-care products including L'Oréal, Kerastase, Redken, Aveda and Fudge range from Australia. Some discounts. Lots of general hair care advice.

WORTH A LOOK: 'Hair Style' section where you click on photos showing models with a range of styles and see what products you could use to achieve the look

DELIVERY: £2 plus 50p per item/1–2 days

Menses.co.uk

Alternative women's sanitary products. Choose from washable menstrual pads, silk sponges or a reusable menstrual cup. All eco-friendly.

WORTH A LOOK: links to interesting related sites including the Museum of Menstruation

DELIVERY: included/14 days

Moltonbrown.co.uk

Luxury own-brand hair, grooming, skin and body care products for men and women from this top London salon.

WORTH A LOOK: 'Chinese remedies' section for unusual skin treatments based on Chinese herbs

DELIVERY: £3.95/7 days

pharmacy2u.co.uk

Online chemist. Private prescriptions catered for plus over-the-counter medicines, healthcare and beauty products and disability aids. Email a pharmacist for online advice.

WORTH A LOOK: useful link to health information sites, including **Embarrassingproblems.co.uk**

DELIVERY: £2.50 on orders up to £30, included over £30, plus free private prescription deliveries/1–3 days

Simplylenses.com

Wide range of contact lenses and solutions at discount prices. Prescription needed before lenses supplied.

WORTH A LOOK: 'Educational' section with information on how the eye works

DELIVERY: included/1–2 days

Thephysiostore.com

Online physiotherapy store selling range of items designed to help alleviate muscle and joint pain. Products include support pillows, heat packs, TENS machines and back supports.

WORTH A LOOK: 'Ask the physio' service – for a charge, a physiotherapist can give a personal consultation by email and suggest products to suit your particular problem

DELIVERY: £3/2 days

Thinknatural.com

'Natural health' site selling aromatherapy oils, vitamin and mineral supplements, Bach flower and homeopathic remedies, plus body-care products and gifts. Wide range of brands.
WORTH A LOOK: 'Pet health' section for natural remedies especially designed for pets
DELIVERY: £2.50 on orders up to £50, or included over/1–3 days

Vitago.co.uk

All-purpose health and beauty store with everything from over-the-counter medicines and toothbrushes to Chanel perfumes and Clarins skincare products.
WORTH A LOOK: 4 'e-mags' on the site with news and articles covering fitness, children, health and lifestyle and beauty
DELIVERY: £2.95/1–2 days

Which? Web Trader round-up

- **Disabilitysupplies.com** all types of independent living support aids
- **Grooming4men.com** men's grooming essentials
- **Haircare4men.com** includes products for and advice on hair loss
- **Herbalnet.co.uk** aromatherapy and massage oils
- **Pitrok.co.uk** natural body-care products including the Tongue Cleaner for bad breath and anti-snoring products
- **Posture.co.uk** suppliers of ergonomic chairs

Home

You may not find on the Internet all the furniture brand names you may expect from the high street. MFI has a site selling a good range, but although Habitat and Ikea both have sites publicising their ranges, at the time of writing they do not sell online. However, established mail-order companies such as McCord and lots of smaller shops selling more unusual items are well represented on the Net.

Bathroomexpress.co.uk

Upgrade your existing bathroom to a luxury one. Whirlpool baths, 'Après-Shower' body driers (basically a hand-drier you can stand under), steam showers and bath pillows. Selection of special-needs bathroom equipment.
WORTH A LOOK: designer toilet seats with motifs from starfish and moons to a clear acrylic seat containing barbed wire!
DELIVERY: 5–10 days/£4.50

Bouchon.co.uk

Stylish accessories for home and garden at the online branch of this mail-order company. Lots of contemporary-looking silver-plated, pewter and aluminium designs. Plenty of ideas for gifts too. Online orders are 5% cheaper than in the standard Bouchon catalogue.
WORTH A LOOK: interesting range of accessories for the 'bar' – silver-plated wine stoppers and a wine thermometer, for instance
DELIVERY: £3.95/2–5 days

Cookcraft.com

Quality cookware and other items for the contemporary kitchen. Mostly leading European brands – Le Creuset, Chartres, Gaggia, Alessi, for instance. Small selection of barbeques and picnic accessories, houseware and storage items too.
WORTH A LOOK: 'International Cuisine' section for cookware designed specifically for Asian, Italian and Spanish dishes
DELIVERY: £2.95/2–3 days

emccord.uk.com

Well-known mail-order catalogue company's online branch.
Modern-style furniture and bedding, plus lamps, cutlery and
glassware, storage, pictures, home office items and a wealth of
other products to deck out your home.
WORTH A LOOK: 'Online Outlet' section for good discounts on
end-of-line items
DELIVERY: £2.95/10 days

Furniture123.co.uk

UK's largest online furniture store claiming savings of up to 30%
off high-street prices. Shop by room by selecting 'children's
furniture', 'kitchen furniture' for example, or use their Product
Finder search facility.
WORTH A LOOK: online furniture magazine to help with
inspiration
DELIVERY: £25 on orders under £300, included over/time depends
on the product but, as an example, a futon takes 2–3 weeks and a
Shaker-style dining table with chairs 6–8 weeks.

Furniturebusters.com

Discount furniture store selling many well-known brands, such
as Stag and Caxton. Browse by the style of furniture you are after
– sections divided into 'modern living', 'traditional living',
'leather', for instance.
WORTH A LOOK: very wide selection of grandfather
clocks
DELIVERY: included in and around London, £50 plus
VAT elsewhere/4–8 weeks

Lakelandlimited.com

'Creative' kitchen gadgets, cookware and other household items.
Lots of things you never knew you needed – a cast-iron bacon
crisper, an electronic pepper mill or an expanding toast rack, for
instance.
WORTH A LOOK: 'Delia's Collection' for Delia Smith-inspired
choice of cookware
DELIVERY: £2.95, or included on orders over £38/2–3 days

Maelstrom.co.uk

Contemporary/designer cool. From kitchenware to furniture, the site is packed with designer names – Alessi, Dualit, Philippe Starck, Ray and Charles Eames. Wide price range so if you cannot afford that Philippe Starck chair, you can go for his juicer instead.

WORTH A LOOK: 'Designers' section for personal histories of the designers featured on the site

DELIVERY: 10% of the order up to £15, then free (furniture charges depend on the item)/5 days

Marksandspencer.co.uk

M&S furniture, lighting, bedlinen, kitchenware and myriad other items for the home available online. A good selection but not the full range. As not all M&S stores stock the furniture or lighting ranges, this site could be useful, for browsing if nothing else.

WORTH A LOOK: if you cannot find what you want you can order the main catalogue online

DELIVERY: £2.95 (furniture delivery is inclusive)/2 days

Mathmos.co.uk

A full selection of lava lamps from the originator of this kitsch design classic. Glitter lamps, fibre-optic lamps, psychedelic moving image space projectors and 'modern' lava lamps with changing colours.

WORTH A LOOK: join the Mathmos lava-lovers club for £9.99 – perks include a free T- shirt, key ring plus a loyalty card to collect points towards gifts

DELIVERY: included/5 days

Mfi.co.uk

Large choice of competitively priced furniture, including a wide home office selection. Pictures show furniture in 'room' settings.

WORTH A LOOK: useful customer tracking option so you can check at what stage your order is in the delivery process

DELIVERY: included/14 days

Oxfam.org

Oxfam's Fair Trade online store sells a range of rugs, throws, cushion covers, wickerware and ceramics all made by small producers around the developing world.

WORTH A LOOK: the 'shop' is part of Oxfam's general site where you can find extensive information on Oxfam's work and what 'Fair Trade' means

DELIVERY: £3.50/14 days

Pineonline.co.uk

Just as the site name implies – buy pine beds, bedroom furniture, tables, chairs and lighting.

WORTH A LOOK: metal beds, mattresses and bedding too

DELIVERY: included/7 days

Showerail.co.uk

Choice of 45 designs for shower curtains, many with an unusual theme – London Underground map or Feng Shui, for example. Natural sponges and other bathroom accessories too.

WORTH A LOOK: 'Bloke's Choice' shopping guide especially for men unsure of what to buy.

DELIVERY: £2.95/2–4 days

Thewhiteco.com

Bedlinen, towels, throws and crockery – all in white. White bedsteads, small tables, drawers and children's furniture too.

WORTH A LOOK: wedding list service

DELIVERY: £3.95–£4.95 depending on the item, furniture is £10–£25/2–4 days

Web-blinds.com

Made-to-measure online window blind company. Stylish, easy-to-use site selling contemporary roller, roman, venetian and vertical blinds at competitive prices. Advice on how to measure up. Free swatch sample service.

WORTH A LOOK: get inspired in the 'Home Ideas Gallery'

DELIVERY: £5/5 days

Wheredidyoubuythat.com

Interesting site with a wide range of products placed in 13 room settings to make up a virtual house and garden. You click into a picture of a room (or the garden) and you can see close-ups and product info on the items in the room. Rooms include 'Nursery', 'Seductive Bedroom' and 'Clean-Cut Bathroom'.

WORTH A LOOK: 'The Crapper' for range of Thomas Crapper replica Victorian sanitaryware

DELIVERY: included/2–3 days

Which? Web Trader round-up

- **Ashbournelinen.co.uk** designer bedding and towels from Descamps, Petite Descamps and Designers Guild
- **Canefurniture-online.co.uk** cane and wicker furniture for conservatory and rest of home
- **Chandeliers.com** crystal chandeliers from the Czech Republic
- **Culliners.co.uk** professional-quality cookware including chefs' knives
- **Decodeli.com** contemporary objects for the home
- **Malkinclocks.co.uk** reproductions of traditional clock designs
- **Rootskitchens.co.uk** fitted kitchen and bedroom furniture
- **Space2.com** home office furniture specialists
- **Thecandleroom.co.uk** candle collection includes aromatherapy candles, incense burners and candleholders
- **Thomas-crapper.com** replica Victorian sanitarywear

Jewellery

It may seem odd to buy jewellery online but as long as the site makes clear the quality of the precious metal, provides a good picture of the item and has a straightforward returns policy, the fact that you cannot touch the item or try it on could be irrelevant. And again, it means no more tramping around from shop to shop.

Although you can choose from a wide range of jewellery, most of the sites are 'discount warehouse'-style operations. This is fine if you want a bargain piece but not so good if you are after a slightly more unusual and individual designer item.

Abooga.com

Gold and silver jewellery for men and women, also designer watches, many at good discounts. Also a range of body jewellery to wear after piercing. Over 30,000 lines available.

WORTH A LOOK: with such a wide choice, the 'shortcut jump' section featuring the best sellers is useful

DELIVERY: included/3–4 days

Cooldiamonds.com

Diamond specialist based in Hatton Garden in London. You choose the style of jewellery from a selection then pick the quality and type of diamond to be set in it.

WORTH A LOOK: 'On sale this week' section for significant discounts

DELIVERY: included/2 days

Gordonstoker.co.uk

Online store of traditional family-run Somerset jewellers. Full jewellery range plus watches.

WORTH A LOOK: handy 'Anniversary List' giving full list of wedding anniversaries and accompanying stones plus zodiac and birthstone details

DELIVERY: included/7 days

Scottish-jewellery.co.uk

Celtic and traditional Scottish jewellery available in white gold, gold, silver and amber. Also Charles Rennie Mackintosh designs.
WORTH A LOOK: range featuring unusual Heathergem 'stone', made from the stems of heather and treated to give a gem-like finish
DELIVERY: £2.59/2–3 days

Thejewellerycatalogue.co.uk

Discount jewellery online superstore with up to 70% off high-street prices. Products divided into 'Gold', 'Diamonds' and 'Antiques'.
WORTH A LOOK: useful guide on making your own price comparisons based on weight of gold in the item of jewellery
DELIVERY: £4.95/2 days

TinyJewellery.com

Fashionable 'fun' jewellery aimed at young women. Toe rings, belly chains, anklets as well as more conservative lines.
WORTH A LOOK: non-metal ranges featuring feathers, snakeskin and beads
DELIVERY: included/7–14 days

Which? Web Trader round-up

- **Argenteus.co.uk** silver and designer jewellery
- **Goldfactory.co.uk** discount 9-carat gold jewellery
- **Irelandsgold.com** Celtic designs
- **Jewellerywarehouse.co.uk** general jewellery site
- **Lioneljacobs.co.uk** site of established jewellery store in Richmond, West London
- **Sovereigndiamonds.com** diamond specialist

Please let us know about your shopping experiences online and of any web sites you would recommend. You can use the report form at the back of the book or email your recommendations to *internetshopping@which.net*

Music, videos and DVDs

Music and videos are very suited to being sold on the Net. The look of the product is unimportant and you do not need to touch or smell or try on before you buy. You are more likely to know exactly what you are getting when you order and you may have read reviews or listened to sample tracks from albums via the site. Competition is strong, so it pays to compare sites. Sites known best for their books are also major music and video sellers. It is also worth looking at US sites for some releases. They can be cheaper but don't automatically presume they will be (see Chapter 5 for more details on buying from abroad).

Downloading music direct from sites is becoming increasingly available. In other words, you don't buy a physical product like a CD. MP3 technology allows the music from a CD to be compressed into a file which can be stored and played back whenever you want. You need an MP3 player to do this – various sites let you download it for free (try **www.mp3.com**). You can use it to listen to samples supplied by the sites, say, or buy single tracks.

101cd.com

Massive collection of titles. Top 40 and major new release CD albums for under £10. Thousands more CDs, DVDs, videos and computer games at discount prices.
WORTH A LOOK: US and Japanese import section
DELIVERY: £1–£4 depending on order/3–5 days

Audiostreet.co.uk

Part of the Streets Online shopping network. Large selection of music, DVDs, videos and games, plus digital music and video section. Delivery charges are included in the price.
WORTH A LOOK: Streets Online Xchange to buy and sell second-hand
DELIVERY: included/1–2 days

Blackstar.co.uk

Latest videos and DVDs, many at 10–20% off.
Worth a look: loyalty award scheme with various
gifts
Delivery: included/2–3 days

Cdnow.com

A US site catering for all musical tastes from gospel to classical.
Videos, DVDs and books. Some good discounts (but remember
customs charges). The site has a European shipping centre so
delivery can be fast.
Worth a look: lots of interviews, news and reviews with a US
bias
Delivery: $6.96 upwards depending on order/2–4 days

Crotchet.co.uk

Classical music specialists also selling jazz, film and world music.
Worth a look: 'Multi-buy' option on some recordings
for a bigger discount
Delivery: £1.50 first item, 50p subsequent items/2–10
days

Crunch.co.uk

Download music specialists. No CDs here – instead you
download the music you want from the site on to your PC.
Underground rather than mainstream music, but interesting to
look at nevertheless to see how future music shopping sites may
operate. Pay by track, from 99p per track.
Worth a look: useful info for beginners on MP3 and digital
music
Delivery: n/a

HMV

Online branch of this established high-street music, DVD and
video store. Huge stock. You can listen to many titles online.
Clear information on stock availability.
Worth a look: 'Coming soon' section for release dates and
details of up-and-coming titles
Delivery: £1 upwards depending on order/3–21 days

Kidscdsandtapes.com

Child-friendly site selling children's tapes and CDs. Action songs, stories, rhymes, lullabies and pop. Cartoon characters and competitions too. Selection of BBC tapes, including Noddy and Teletubbies.

WORTH A LOOK: party section for children's party music

DELIVERY: 30p upwards depending on order/2 days

Lookmusic.com

Sheet and book music, musical instruments and accessories. Chart CDs too.

WORTH A LOOK: second-hand section for buying instruments from private individuals

DELIVERY: 50p upwards depending on order/3–5 days

Ministryofsound.com

Look at the online store on this clubbers' site for good choice of own-label dance music CDs. Trance, techno, pop house, UK garage and more.

WORTH A LOOK: various clubbers' guides on the main site

DELIVERY: £1 upwards depending on order/3–28 days

Moviem.co.uk

World cinema and cult films on video and DVD. Specialists in hard-to-find films.

WORTH A LOOK: the Moviemail Top 30 films of all time

DELIVERY: £1 per video, DVDs included/1–2 days

Reddingtonsrarerecords.co.uk

Rare music on vinyl and CD. Specialists in Rock 'n' Roll, Country, Soul, R&B, Punk and Heavy Metal. Collection includes rare Beatles, Rolling Stones and Jimi Hendrix releases. Estimated stock of two million 45s.

WORTH A LOOK: browse the catalogue or enter an artist's name in the search box to see some titles to remind you of your youth!

DELIVERY: £1 for singles and CDs, £2 for albums plus 50p each additional item/2–3 days

Thebebopshop.com

Specialists in swing, bebop, hardbop and classic modern jazz recordings. Extensive selection plus links to the best-known jazz sites.

WORTH A LOOK: monthly spotlight artist with reduced prices for that artist's albums that month

DELIVERY: £1 for one disc and 50p per subsequent disc/6-8 days

Virginmega.com

Virgin Megastore's US site has a vast collection of CDs, videos and DVDs (UK site under preparation). Good place to try out transAtlantic shopping as international shipping details are very clear.

WORTH A LOOK: 'Virgin Jamcast' free service sending you downloads of your chosen genres of music every week

DELIVERY: $7.99 upwards depending on order/7–14 days

Which? Web Trader round-up

- **Axemail.com** specialists in new and second-hand guitars, amps, recording equipment, woodwind and brass
- **Bensonsworld.co.uk** established video and DVD store
- **Burbs.co.uk** music from UK underground rock bands
- **Chamberlainmusic.com** musical instruments and sheet music
- **Choicesdirect.co.uk** every video and DVD on UK release
- **Dawsons.co.uk** leading musical instrument store
- **Musicscotland.com** Celtic music from Scotland, Ireland and beyond
- **Nightcafe.co.uk** specialists in relaxing late-night sounds, including electronic, acoustic and early music
- **Seaford-music.co.uk** international classical music store specialising in providing classical music from Europe, Australasia and the USA
- **Ukdvdrentals.co.uk** rent or buy the latest DVDs

Pets

As a nation Britons spend an average of £86 a year on their pets so it's no wonder that pet-care sites have been amongst the fastest growing on the Net.

Pets can easily be pampered via the Internet. There are sites selling all manner of pet paraphernalia from fur conditioner to 'designer' bedding, as well as the more run-of-the-mill pet food and cat litter. You can insure your pet's health, take steps to make sure your pet is returned to you if he or she goes missing and, when the end comes, bury him or her under a dignified headstone.

Animail.co.uk

Online pet shop stocking over 2,000 pet-related products from a 'luxurious fur yuppy cat bed' to fish food. Pet carriers, cages (or 'housing units'), straw and hay for bedding, leads and harnesses and pet toys too.

WORTH A LOOK: lots of advice on training animals and dealing with difficult behaviour

DELIVERY: £2.95 or included over £40/2–3 days

Bouldercraft.com

Garden pet memorials made from Yorkshire boulders. Natural shapes to blend in with rest of garden. Alternatively, choose traditional-looking granite or marble headstones.

WORTH A LOOK: no extra features on the site but clear pictures of the memorials help you choose

DELIVERY: included/30 days

Datapet.co.uk

Pet security. Datapet sells a security kit (a tag with Datapet's 24-hr telephone number on it). If your pet gets lost, the person who finds it contacts Datapet and they will help reunite you. The person who finds the pet gets rewarded in cash by Datapet. You can also put a photo of your missing pet on the 'Lost and Found' section of the site.

WORTH A LOOK: pet insurance for sale too

DELIVERY: included/7 days

Headstartpets.co.uk

All natural products for pets. GM-free and organic foods and supplements plus natural shampoos, flea treatments, herbal medicines, conditioners and medical products.

WORTH A LOOK: 'Magnotherapy' range of magnetic collars for cats and dogs designed to relieve arthritis pain

DELIVERY: £2, or included on orders over £35/7 days

Netfysh.com

Instant pets online. Not pets in the traditional sense but 'grow-your-own' mini-crustaceans. Choose from Triops (look like tiny horseshoe crabs) or sea-monkeys (brine shrimps). Add water and they start to emerge. Popular with children.

WORTH A LOOK: chat forums to exchange pet tales

DELIVERY: £2/14 days

Pets-pyjamas.co.uk

General pet provision site but with some good gift ideas for both pet and owner. Wide range of pet toys and treats plus, for pet lovers, animal-inspired clothing and accessories.

WORTH A LOOK: 'Pet Jokes' section to see the latest pet humour
DELIVERY: £2.95 for orders under £35, included over/2–5 days

Rspcashop.co.uk

Unusual and reasonably priced range of pet products and goodies from the Royal Society for the Prevention of Cruelty to Animals (RSPCA) with the added bonus that you are supporting the charity by buying from the site. Range includes ergonomic dog feeder (so your dog eats in supreme comfort), dog 'dry bag' to dry and clean your dog after wet walks and 'I love cats' feeding mat.

WORTH A LOOK: the main RSPCA site is full of useful pet care info
DELIVERY: £3.60/14 days

Phones

Sites selling mobile phones proliferate on the Internet. Shop around and you should be able to find some good deals on high-street prices. The best sites are those that clearly explain the different tariffs so that you can easily work out the best deal for you. Phone sites do, however, have a tendency to talk to the converted, so if you are a complete novice you could find yourself at sea – look at a few sites until you find one that provides you with the information you need to make an informed purchase.

Axex.co.uk

Mobile phone accessories. Click on the brand of phone you have and up comes a range of accessories for it from cases to hands-free units. Batteries and 'fun' items such as cartoon-character phone cases too.

WORTH A LOOK: 'Why the hell should I want a . . . ?' section for lowdown on selected accessories
DELIVERY: included/2–4 days

Callcrazy.com

Online phonecard shop. Vodaphone, Orange, One2One, Virgin, BTCellnet and a large selection of international cards.

WORTH A LOOK: 'Card Wizard' helps you find the best international phonecard for you by comparing costs to your chosen country between cards
DELIVERY: details of your chosen phonecard (PIN, serial number, access numbers etc) are emailed as soon as credit card details are cleared

Carphonewarehouse.com

Huge choice of mobile phones and everything you could need to go with them.

WORTH A LOOK: 'Encyclopedia mobilia' section for lots of useful info on buying a mobile and how they work
DELIVERY: included/3–4 days

Justphones.co.uk

All the latest phones including WAP phones. Informative site
with good advice on choosing a phone.

WORTH A LOOK: online phone auction for the chance
of cheap deals

DELIVERY: included/1 day

Miah-telecom.co.uk

Neatly organised phone site packed with info, although may be
more useful for those who already know something about the
phone they want.

WORTH A LOOK: useful 'tariff calculator' to help you
work out the tariff or network to suit your needs

DELIVERY: included/ 1–2 days

Talkingshop.co.uk

All the latest phones plus well-presented information on tariffs.
Look at the Buyers' Guide for useful explanations of various
aspects of mobile phone terminology.

WORTH A LOOK: 'News' section for details of latest phones and
tariffs

DELIVERY: included/1–2 days

Property

You cannot yet exchange and complete on a house purchase on the Net but plenty of sites exist to help you find a house or flat. The sites are similar and generally have databases of properties – you key in your requirements and the site comes up with properties that fit them. Be prepared to be disappointed, however – there is not yet detailed national coverage. You may type in your requirements knowing there are properties where you want and the search will come up with nothing. Sites tend to depend on estate agents registering their properties with them. You may fare better looking at the web sites of local estate agents; these are proliferating.

The general property sites can be useful for helping you organise your move – from finding removal firms to deciding on the electricity supplier for your new home.

Assertahome.com

Search this database for a house or flat to rent or buy. Countrywide, including Wales and Scotland. You key in the place name or postcode of the area you are interested in, e.g. Cardiff or SW2, press 'go' and a list of properties in that area will come up. If you find one that suits you, you contact the estate agent by phone or email. Details of local removal firms, solicitors and surveyors available.

WORTH A LOOK: registration service for updates by email on new properties coming on the market

Fish4homes.co.uk

Details on over 200,000 homes online plus insurance, mortgage, legal and removal advice and contacts.

WORTH A LOOK: 'property jargon' buster to help you through the buying jungle

French-property.com

If you are thinking of buying a holiday home in France, this site could prove useful. Database of properties for sale throughout France. Search by region or by linking up with local estate agents.

WORTH A LOOK: rentals section for temporary holiday homes

Ihavemoved.com

Save yourself time ringing up all the businesses and utility companies to which you need to give a change of address by keying in the appropriate details on this site – it does it for you for free. The site can also take care of starting or stopping gas, electricity and water services.

WORTH A LOOK: link to **Homepro.com**, a site with a large database of decorators, builders, plumbers etc to work on your new home

Propertybroker.com

Properties for sale privately throughout the London-M25 area. Large, clear series of pictures for each property showing inside and outside. No estate agents' fees so a useful shop window for sellers. You contact the seller direct to arrange a viewing.

WORTH A LOOK: the photos are large enough to give a decent impression of the properties (useful if only just to snoop around other peoples' décor)

Reallymoving.com

As with most other property sites, estate agents provide the site with details of homes. This database boasts 50,000 properties. Instant online quotes for solicitors, cleaning companies, removal firms etc, plus lots of moving advice.

WORTH A LOOK: 'Mini Move' section for low-cost removals for small loads

Underoneroof.com

Stylish-looking property site which is part of the Associated Newspaper Group.

WORTH A LOOK: 'HomeCheck' service links you to a security company that carries out property reports covering aspects such as neighbourhood noise and nuisance, litter, risk from flooding, schools and youth clubs, traffic and parking

Upmystreet.com

A different kind of property site. You cannot buy or sell via this site, but instead you can build up a picture of the neighbourhood in which you are interested. Site provides information on local schools, shops, crime, property prices and local councils

WORTH A LOOK: find out about the area you live in now by keying in your postcode or town. Good way of testing accuracy of information

Which? Web Trader round-up

- **Flat-sharer.com** find your ideal flat-mate
- **Froglet.com** services for landlords including downloadable tenancy agreements
- **Lmn8.com** Internet property service eliminating property agents

---

You may find the following Which? titles useful when buying or selling property, renting or organising your move: *Which? Way to Buy, Sell and Move House, Which? Way to Buy, Own and Sell a Flat,* and *The Which? Guide to Renting and Letting.*

Religious products

Sites in the USA, not surprisingly perhaps, offer by far the best range of religious merchandise. You could buy your rosary beads and statuettes of the Virgin Mary from sites such as **TotallyCatholic.com**. You could visit **Holylandmall.com** for Jewish, Christian and Muslim merchandise. However, many of these sites are not geared up for international orders. Below are some sites that do ship to the UK (although how fast is another matter).

Christianbook.com

'Your headquarters for everything Christian . . . for less' goes the site slogan. US 'Christian superstore' selling not just books on different aspects of Christianity but cross-design traditional quilts, plates and dishes with quotes from the Bible, Adam and Eve figurines, the Lord's Prayer pillowcases and more. International orders by sea-mail only, so be prepared for a long wait.

WORTH A LOOK: the Bible Message Camera which automatically places a quote from the Bible on each exposure

DELIVERY: $5 for orders up to $25 or 20% of cost of order for above this/2–5 months

Divineimages.com

Spiritual products from this US site. Personal altars for worship at home or in the office, religious figurines from many cultures including mini-Buddhas, candles to enhance meditation and books on spiritual subjects.

WORTH A LOOK: Legends and Stories section for the history behind a range of religious images

DELIVERY: the site ships internationally but you need to email the company saying what you want to order so it can calculate the cost and give an estimate of time

Which? Web Trader round-up

- **Gospelstorehouse.co.uk** books with a Christian theme
- **Kingdomfaith.com** web site of the Kingdom Faith Church

For a fuller list of Which? Web Traders,
see Part 3, or go to www.which.net/webtrader

Sportswear and equipment

Football gear and casual sportswear is widely available on the Internet. Cycling and outdoor wear and equipment can also be purchased. You may need to search harder for sites selling non-mainstream sportswear and equipment but our listings should help you get what you want.

9feet.com

Outdoor clothing and adventure sports equipment site catering for camping, climbing, hiking, mountain biking and snow sports needs. All the major brands represented including Lowe alpine, Karrimor and Merrell.

WORTH A LOOK: 'Making Tracks' magazine-style section with news and features on adventure sports
DELIVERY: £3 (included over £50)/3–5 days

Arsenal.co.uk

Most leading football teams have their own web sites. This site gives an example of the kind of merchandise you can buy. Latest kits plus footballs, boots, tracksuits, T-shirts, curtains, wallpaper, watches and anything else that can sport the team logo

WORTH A LOOK: a whole 'Baby' section with everything from bibs to sleepsuits
DELIVERY: £3/ 28 days

Bicyclenet.co.uk

Bikes to suit all ages and abilities, many at discount prices.

WORTH A LOOK: good selection of children's bikes
DELIVERY: £6.50/4 days

Cricshop.com

Online shop of informative cricket web site, **cricinfo.com**.
Cricket videos and books as well as a range of equipment.
WORTH A LOOK: the main site is full of in-depth analysis, statistics,
match updates and coaching tips
DELIVERY: included/14 days

Discountsports.co.uk

Big names including Adidas, Nike and Puma at discount prices.
Trainers, clothing, balls, bags and more.
WORTH A LOOK: the site offers a 'Collectpoint' service for
busy people who can't be at home to take in their order.
DELIVERY: included/7 days

Exercise.co.uk

'Exercise, Fitness and Leisure' is a home shopping channel
selling a broad range of exercise equipment from rowing
machines to steps and weight-training gear.
WORTH A LOOK: charts to measure your fitness in the
'how fit are you' section
DELIVERY: included/4–7 days

Fade-fashion.com

Male and female golfwear with a contemporary designer look.
No diamond V-neck jumpers here. Moody black all-in-ones,
stylish zip-up tops and sporty lightweight skirts.
WORTH A LOOK: links to useful golf web sites such as
www.golf.com
DELIVERY: £3.50/7 days

Fishingwarehouse.co.uk

Online tackle shop catering for all types of fishing. Search under
Carp, Coarse, Game/Fly, Match, Predator and Sea.
WORTH A LOOK: big reductions on rods in the 'Scoops' section
DELIVERY: £5.50 up to £50, £10.50 over/3 days

Kitbag.com

Football shirts of UK and international teams. Retro 1960s and 1970s shirts. Rugby, cricket and Formula 1 clothing and a good selection of equipment.

WORTH A LOOK: 'Teamwear' section for personalised team football kits

DELIVERY: included/next day

Newitts.com

One of largest UK mail-order suppliers of sports equipment. Caters not just for mass-market sports but also more unusual sports such as archery, lacrosse and weight training.

WORTH A LOOK: play a penalty shoot-out game online

DELIVERY: included/next day

Theproshop.co.uk

Claims to be the UK's largest golf online store. Everything imaginable to do with golf. Clubs, balls, bags and putters plus clothing and other accessories.

Worth a look: 10% off first orders from the 'proshopwoman' section

DELIVERY: included/3 days

Rockrun.com

Specialist equipment and clothing for climbing enthusiasts. Crampons, ice picks, maps and a wide choice of lightweight and insulated clothing.

WORTH A LOOK: link to **ukclimbing.com**, a climbers' web site packed with climbing information

DELIVERY: £5/1–2 days

Singletrack.co.uk

Specialists in BMX and mountain bikes. Lots of clothing and accessories too.

WORTH A LOOK: special feature where you can build your own bike online out of various parts

DELIVERY: £1/2days

Sportsmart.co.uk

General online sports store selling clothing, shoes and a limited range of equipment. Puma, Reebok, Adidas, New Balance, Umbro and other brand names.

WORTH A LOOK: many sale items delivered free

DELIVERY: £3/2days

Sportsshoes.com

Online store of specialist Yorkshire sports shoe shop, SportsShoes Unlimited. Training shoes, golf, running, basketball and racket sports shoes amongst others.

WORTH A LOOK: 'Big foot' section for larger sizes

DELIVERY: £3/3–5 days

Tennisnuts.com

Specialists in racket sports including tennis, badminton and squash. All the brand names from Dunlop to Wilson available. Clothing and shoes as well as rackets. Table tennis, snooker, fitness and running equipment too.

WORTH A LOOK: lots of useful product reviews and links to tennis sites

DELIVERY: £4 on orders under £100, included over/2–4 days

Troutfishing.co.uk

Fishing tackle site with wide range of trout and salmon tied flies plus fly boxes and other fly fishing accessories.

WORTH A LOOK: trout fishery directory – find a fishery near you

DELIVERY: included/2–3 days

Upandunder.co.uk

Specialist outdoor equipment retailer dedicated to canoeing, caving, climbing and walking. Everything from stove spares to inflatable rafts.

WORTH A LOOK: 'Bargain Bin' for cut-price equipment plus a 'Resources' section for listings of outdoor events and clubs

DELIVERY: £2.50–£5, included for goods over £400/3–5 days

Wimbledon.org

Official Wimbledon merchandise. No tennis rackets here but lots of clothing, bags, towels, books and videos for Wimbledon fans.
WORTH A LOOK: Wimbledon facts and figures on the main site
DELIVERY: included/28 days

Which? Web Trader round-up

- **Balls-fore-golf.co.uk** new golf balls and lake balls
- **Boat-net.co.uk** chandlery online
- **Cyclestore.co.uk** bikes and accessories
- **Golfshopper.co.uk** all types of golf equipment
- **Jackfish.net** Yorkshire fishing tackle shop online
- **Kinetics.org.uk** unusual and bespoke bikes, including folding and electronic
- **Skatepool.com** skateboarding products
- **Sportsbras.co.uk** sports bras plus women's sports underwear
- **Tackandski.co.uk** horse riding and skiing equipment

Tickets and travel

Ticket sales of all sorts are supremely suited to the Internet, perhaps because there is no tangible product and none of the usual problems with delivery. Good deals are snapped up quickly so when you see a bargain, speed is of the essence. It pays to shop around too. Remember that although the Internet allows you to be your own travel agent and check factors such as flight availability and timetables yourself, if you are pushed for time, doing your own travel research may not be your best option. It may be more practical for you to choose a site that does a lot of the work for you.

Aloud.com

Live music concert ticket site owned by the Emap magazine group. Mainly rock/pop. Extra features include a festival guide, reviews and entertainment news. Booking fee and ticket postage charged.

WORTH A LOOK: 'Selling fast' section for the tickets to get a move on and buy

Bargainholidays.com

Late-availability cut-price package trips. Over 70,000 offers available. Flight-only and car-hire deals too.
WORTH A LOOK: useful destination guides to help you make your choice

Expedia.co.uk

Major travel ticket site from Microsoft. Search under flights, hotels, cars, holiday shop, destinations, business travel and maps. Lots of extra features including fare price-comparison facility.
WORTH A LOOK: 'Fare tracker' service for weekly email updates on fares

Ferrysavers.co.uk

Tickets for ferry crossings for cars to and from Ireland and the continent. Cheapest fare they can find on the day you want to travel is displayed along with the fare closest to the time you want to travel.

WORTH A LOOK: regular competitions to win tickets

Flynow.com

Cheap flights from over 40 of the world's scheduled airlines. 'Etickets' booking system means you are not sent tickets – everything is on the airline's computer.

WORTH A LOOK: visa and passport service

Go-fly.com

Bargain flight company – ex-subsidiary of British Airways. Up to 50% off late-availability flights.

WORTH A LOOK: special deals for car hire, insurance and hotels

Gobycoach.com

National Express coach web site. Book coach journey tickets to UK and European destinations. Airport service and coach transport to events available too.

WORTH A LOOK: short-break package trips by coach

Holidayautos.co.uk

Car rental broker with links to car rental companies all over the world. Price-match guarantee means they will match any cheaper price you find.

WORTH A LOOK: 'late deals' section for last-minute bargains

Lastminute.com

Late deals on flights, holidays and hotels, plus theatre, concert, sports and events tickets.

WORTH A LOOK: 'What you can do next weekend' section with a large selection of ideas and deals

Theaa.co.uk

Book accommodation direct via the AA's site. Database of over 8,000 UK hotels, B&Bs, pubs and inns.

WORTH A LOOK: 'Special offer' section for 'exclusive' deals for AA web site users

Thetrainline.com

Book train tickets for anywhere in the UK. Up-to-date information on timetables and ticket types.

WORTH A LOOK: 'Favourite journey' facility for travellers who regularly use the same route – no need to input the same details every time you book

Ticketmaster.co.uk

Leading entertainment and sports ticketing company. Buy tickets for all sorts of entertainment from theatre to rugby league games to exhibitions to clubs. Booking fee charged on some tickets.

WORTH A LOOK: search by venue facility gives a rundown of events coming up at venues all over the UK

Warnervillage.co.uk

Online box office for Warner Village cinemas. See what's on at your local Warner cinema, read the review and book the ticket all online at this site.

WORTH A LOOK: links to a range of film sites including *Hollywood Reporter* for entertainment gossip

Which? Web Trader round-up

- **Eurotours.co.uk** city-breaks specialist
- **Flipflops.co.uk** summer villas and apartments
- **Goplaces.co.uk** online luggage sales
- **Outdoor-leisure.com** camping and outdoor products
- **Instant-holidays.com** over 70,000 holidays on its database
- **Leisurehunt.com** Internet accommodation service for luxury hotels to B&Bs
- **Snow-line.co.uk** ski and snowboarding holidays
- **Travelstore.com** business travel specialist

Holiday Which? **says:**

For flights and car hire, the Internet is a great place to book online. You can compare prices without having to make lots of phone calls and are likely to get more detail about your travel arrangements than from a travel agent.

For accommodation, it is harder to find the same hotel on different web sites. This makes price comparison difficult, but location maps and pictures and detailed lists of facilities mean that you can be reassured about your choice.

With package holidays it is less clear cut. Most of the sites offering holidays from the big tour operators (including their own) don't allow you to book online, so you will often end up having to ring or email an agent or tour operator to confirm details anyway. The Internet may be a useful tool for allowing you to do some initial research to compare prices, but for the full range of what's available you should consider other sources of information too.

For a useful list of travel web sites, try the directory **www.travelworld.co.uk**

For further information on how to organise your holiday online, see *Holiday Which?* Spring 2001.

Toys and games

From traditional metal toys to the latest TV-inspired fads you can find what you want (or what the child wants) without too much trouble on the Internet. Delivery charges can be high if you order more than one item, so check the total price. If you are ordering at Christmas, get your order in as early as you can – just as with the high-street shops the Christmas rush for the season's most desirable toys results in heavily diminished stocks for some items.

Dawson-and-son.com

Long-established (in Internet terms) site with over 300 traditional-style toys and games. Specialist in wooden toys.
WORTH A LOOK: 'Stocking Filler' section for cheap and unusual but still tasteful ideas
DELIVERY: £3.95, included if order over £75/2 days

Elc.co.uk

Site for the Early Learning Centre. Wide selection of imaginative educational toys. A huge choice of arts and crafts, music making, construction and activity toys but not the site to choose if you want the current fads.
WORTH A LOOK: impressive range of children's sports and outdoor equipment.
DELIVERY: £2.95/3 days

Hamleys.co.uk

The online version of the world-famous London toy shop. Not a very exciting site design, but boasts unusual traditional toys and classics, plus a reasonable selection of more current toys.
WORTH A LOOK: good range of high-quality traditional metal soldiers
DELIVERY: £3.95/3–5 days.

In2toys.com

Specialist discount online toy site with promise of at least a 30% saving on recommended retail prices. Stock is fairly limited so you may not be able to get toys from the latest 'must-have' lists. Bear in mind that other toy sites offer reductions on some ranges too, so in2toys may not always be the cheapest.
WORTH A LOOK: reduced Pokémon merchandise
DELIVERY: £3 first item, £1 each additional item/7–10 days

Jokeshopfun.com

Everything to do with jokes, masks and magic tricks. Great for more unusual gifts for adults as well as children.
WORTH A LOOK: selection of 'rude' tricks such as the electronic fart machine
DELIVERY: £1/3 days

Klikit.co.uk

Scale-model kits galore, most with a military theme. Tanks, helicopters, cars and sci-fi kits. Suitable for older children as an element of skill is required. £15 minimum order.
WORTH A LOOK: if you have a request for a particular model not on the site, email Klikit and it will look out for it
DELIVERY: included/3–5 days

Krucialkids.com

Educational toys, particularly for pre-schoolers. Emphasis on toys that strive to meet the developmental needs of young children. Toy categories are divided into 'skills' – for example, 'hand-eye co-ordination' and 'counting' .
WORTH A LOOK: each toy description is accompanied by a 'developmental value' summary
DELIVERY: £1.95 under £20, £3.95 for £20–£59.99, included £60 and over/7–10 days

Online-hobbies.co.uk

The Dinosaur Shop on this model-making site offers a wide range of dinosaur models and self-assembly kits for the dinosaur-crazed child. Selection includes snapping jaws T-rex action figures, cast-your-own dinosaur skeleton kits, inflatable dinosaurs and models based on the BBC's *Walking with Dinosaurs* series.

WORTH A LOOK: dinosaur posters and books

DELIVERY: priced by weight – cost shown at checkout/3–7 days

Sciencemuseumstore.com

Fascinating range of products from the Science Museum's catalogue. The site is in its infancy and only 100 products are available from the 300 that appear in the standard catalogue. Worth keeping an eye on.

WORTH A LOOK: interesting selection of robotic toys such as the 'Climb-a-Tron' climbing robotic toy

DELIVERY: £3.99/3 days

Senatoys.co.uk

Specialists in quality die-cast toys and models for children and collectors. Huge range of tractors, lorries, diggers and other vehicles. Also traditional wooden dolls' houses, garages, farm sets and castles.

WORTH A LOOK: full range of Thomas the Tank Engine die-cast trains – even the most obscure characters.

DELIVERY: £2.50 up to £10, £3.50 for £10–£50, included over £50/28 days.

Teddy-bear-uk.com

Site devoted to quality teddy bears. Heirloom teddies by all the major names in the teddy bear business from Steiff to Merrythought. Also traditional golliwogs, Paddington and Rupert models.

WATCH OUT FOR: Her Majesty Queen Elizabeth the Queen Mother collectors' teddy at £125

DELIVERY: £3.50 up to £50, included over/2 days

Toyzone.co.uk

Colourful site geared towards children as well as adults. Browse by department – for example, boys' action, pre-school collectables – or search by specific toy or by age group.
WORTH A LOOK: 'Hot' toy department with all the latest fads
DELIVERY: £2.50 first item, £1 each additional item/2 days

Woolworths.co.uk

Not the largest selection, but good for character toys and games. Delivery deadline longer than for most other toy sites.
WORTH A LOOK: 'School Stuff' section for a wide range of character backpacks displaying everything from Bob the Builder to Barbie
DELIVERY: £1.50 under £15 or £2.95 over/10 days

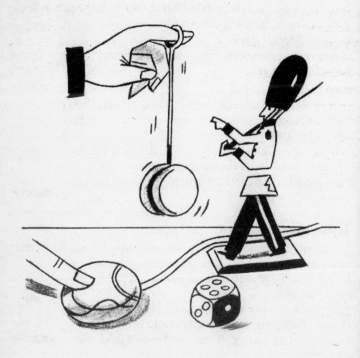

Thepartystore.co.uk

Kids' party paraphernalia including costumes, magic tricks,
inflatables and balloons, games, themed tableware, face masks
and mini-presents for party bags.

WORTH A LOOK: 'Party Store Pages' section to help you
find local sources for bouncy castles, marquees, caterers
and clowns

DELIVERY: £2.95 up to £70, included over/2–5 days

Which? Web Trader round-up

- **Activekid.co.uk** outdoor activity toys
- **Buckiebears.mcmail.com** hand-crafted mohair teddies
- **Funandgamestoyshop.co.uk** site of family-run toy shop
  near Bristol
- **Grannie-annie.co.uk** Beanie Babies specialist
- **Littlebylittle.co.uk** handmade dolls' house miniatures
- **Littlewonders.co.uk** toy site specialising in 0-7 year olds
- **Malltraders.com/strongcrafts** the place to buy rag dolls,
  puppets and wallhangings
- **Toycentre.com** toy site of Merretts toy chain

Wine and beer

The world of wine is at your fingertips on the Net. Not only can you visit producers' sites around the world with merely a mouse click or two, but a few well-spent minutes browsing on a Sunday evening could yield some significant bargains for your cellar as well as expand your knowledge of wine.

BBR.com

An impressive and efficient site which has built on its early start on the Internet. Berry Bros is not just about classic wines – the list is as contemporary as you could wish and as extensive. Upmarket certainly, but not necessarily prohibitive. Much useful and well-informed content too.

WORTH A LOOK: wine school, wine club, tastings and dinners

DELIVERY: £7.50 for orders under £100/6 days

Bibendum-wine.co.uk

Although you don't get to see pictures of bottles of wine, the Bibendum site is a quick way to access this North London company's innovative and wide-ranging list.

WORTH A LOOK: En primeur/regional offers, often unrivalled tasting events

DELIVERY: £10 for orders under £75

Buywineonline.co.uk

Wines at supermarket prices. Order by the bottle or case or create your own mixed case.

WORTH A LOOK: gift selection includes champagne and chocolates and port and cheese boxes

DELIVERY: £4.95/5 days

For more online-only wine merchants and details of independent and high-street merchants with web sites, see *The Which? Wine Guide 2001*. This award-winning annual guide explores the vast range of wine available to the British consumer.

Chateauonline.co.uk

The first real pureplay Internet wine merchant. Paris-based chateauonline maintains an active, visually busy site with 1,400 wines chosen by sommelier Jean-Michel Deluc. Online forms and animated wine advice should satisfy wine enthusiasts.
WORTH A LOOK: seasonal offers, gifts
DELIVERY: £5.99/7 days

Laithwaites.com

The biggest of the bunch, Laithwaites (formerly Bordeaux Direct) has many loyal followers and sells more wine direct than any other merchant by a long chalk. Tony Laithwaite's idiosyncratic style helps wine lovers become involved in his buying forays.
WORTH A LOOK: Wines of the week
DELIVERY: £4.99/one week

Majestic.com

Already expert in case sales – Majestic uses the web to link directly to stores rather than central delivery, so you can retain a personal link with your local branch via email if necessary. The site is fast, busy and easy to use, and the wines, as always, up to scratch.
WORTH A LOOK: Managers' Choice selections
DELIVERY: Free/7 days (2 hours slots possible)

Oddbins.com

From the wackiest wine merchant on the high street, a relatively restrained web site but crammed with interesting and mind-expanding wines.
WORTH A LOOK: Home delivery of over-heavy cases of champagnes – plus 20% off
DELIVERY: £4.99/4 days

Virginwines.com

A staggering 17,500 wines available; closer inspection reveals 500 recommended wines which Virgin stocks and guarantees swift delivery of. Although new to wine, the Virgin list is respectable, the site fast but aesthetically challenged.
WORTH A LOOK: the original Virgin Wine Wizard that helps to match wines to your specific tastes
DELIVERY: £4.99/7 days

Waitrose.com

Waitrose Wine Direct gives you access to the award-winning
Waitrose wine range, particularly if you don't have a branch
nearby. The site is functional more than inspiring.
WORTH A LOOK: monthly mixed cases at varying price points,
monthly recommended Fine Wines
DELIVERY: £4.50 for orders under £75. 7–10 days

Beer

Traditional ways of buying beer are dominated by the major
players – multinational brewing giants and large-scale distributors
– but the low overheads and direct-marketing possibilities offered
by e-commerce means that small, independent brewers and
retailers can now get a foothold in the marketplace, as some of
these sites demonstrate. This has to be welcome news both for real
ale enthusiasts and for consumers generally.

It is also easier than ever to buy all those wonderful
Continental beers without the need for a trip abroad. Several
British online retailers stock good selections of Belgian and
German beers, but why not go direct to source? Many overseas
beer retailers can deliver to the UK and nearly all speak English.

Many breweries are also going online to sell their products
direct to the end user. These range from the major names such as
Theakston (**www.theakston.com**) to small independent
brewers such as Badger (**www.badgerdirect.com**), and the
Isle of Skye Brewery (**skyebrewery.com**). These sites also tend
to sell lots of branded merchandise, so make a good source of
gifts for the beer-lover in your life.

On the downside, the small players cannot offer the same
economies of scale, and cases of beer can incur significant
delivery charges due to their weight. But isn't it worth the cost
for the possibility of drinking fine cask or bottle-conditioned real
ales in the comfort of your own home? It is also worth
remembering that most of the major supermarkets are going
online. Many of them stock good ranges of beer these days, and
not just the big-name brands.

Aleontap.co.uk

Claims to be the first online UK retailer of cask-conditioned ales, selling beers in 5-, 10- and 20-litre containers (perfect for parties). Run by a real-ale enthusiast for real-ale enthusiasts, includes many less common beers alongside some big names.
WORTH A LOOK: if they don't stock the beer you want, they will try to get it for you
DELIVERY: free in Hereford and Worcester area, otherwise £10 per container/next day for orders received by 3pm

Alestore.co.uk

Over 200 British, Belgian and German beers, many from small independent breweries and micro-breweries. Includes tasting notes and background information on breweries. Variety gift packs available.
WORTH A LOOK: unusual regional Belgian beers and German lagers
DELIVERY: £6.75 for first case, £2.95 for subsequent cases/2 days

Badgerdirect.com

Plenty of information on the past and present of Dorset's Badger brewery, plus the opportunity to buy the full range of beers and a wide selection of branded merchandise. Prices include p&p
WORTH A LOOK: free e-cards – beer-themed greetings for any occasion
DELIVERY: free/ 5 working days

Belgianshop.com

Hundreds of Belgian beers, from Abbey and Trappist beers through to fruit beers and lambic ales. Also sells a vast selection of beer paraphernalia. Not very easy to navigate and prices in US dollars.
WORTH A LOOK: for every Belgian beer there is a special glass, and many of them are on sale here
DELIVERY: prices calculated per order, depend on size of order and delivery address/12 days

Enjoyment.co.uk

Not one for serious beer enthusiasts: features only the major
labels, and beer is included in same category as alcopops. But
prices at least 10 per cent lower than high street. Current order
value is always displayed on screen. Mixed cases available.
WORTH A LOOK: some substantial discounts and special offers
DELIVERY: £4.99 for every 5 cases (or part of 5 cases)/5 working
days

Heaton Beer (www.morduebrewery.com)

Online outlet for Mordue Brewery, selling the brewery's own
award-winning beers alongside a good range of other bottle-
conditioned British ales. Also a limited selection of Belgian and
German beers.
WORTH A LOOK: a good source of hard-to-find unusual bottle-
conditioned real ales
DELIVERY: rates depend on size of order/10 days

Lastorders.com

Wide range of every kind of drink plus drinking paraphernalia
and gifts. Not an inspired selection for the discerning drinker but
there are a few gems among the big-name brands (e.g.
Hoegaarden, Rebellion Blonde, Tom Wood Jolly Ploughman).
WORTH A LOOK: corporate service – ideal for office parties!
DELIVERY: £3.99 per 2 cases (or part of 2 cases)/next day for orders
before 5pm

Realbeerbox.com

Online off-sales department of the Plough and Harrow pub.
Combines a serious love of beer with a whimsical approach to
selling it. High dependence on graphics means it is not the
easiest site to navigate. Online ordering 'in testing' at time of
going to press; gifts and memorabilia also 'coming soon'.
WORTH A LOOK: esoteric real ales with names like Old Legover,
Ripon Jewel, Gothic Ale and Monkey Wrench
DELIVERY: prices on application/next day

Skyebrewery.co.uk

Web presence of the Isle of Skye brewery, offering the full range of beers in mixed or single-style cases. Also a range of gifts and clothes.

WORTH A LOOK: these award-winning ales are not widely available, so make the most of this site

DELIVERY: £10 per case of beer, £1 per merchandise item/ 7 days

Theakstons.com

A slick, easy-to-use site from the famous Yorkshire brewer. Beer sold by the case in bottles or cans; mixed cases available. Cost of delivery is included in the price.

WORTH A LOOK: a wide range of branded giftware

DELIVERY: free/10 days

Which? Web Trader round up

- **Art-of-brewing.co.uk** everything for homebrewers and winemakers

Part 3

A Guide to Which? Web Traders

This list is intended only as a guide to the members of the Which? Web Trader scheme. It was correct at the time of going to press, but as traders are joining the scheme on a daily basis you should check the current list on the Which? Web Trader web site at www.which.net/webtrader

The logo does not imply that Which? or any of its associate companies recommend the goods or services offered or the customer service provided by the trader outside the areas covered by the Code of Practice.

The Which? Web Trader Scheme

The Which? Web Trader Scheme is an Internet accreditation scheme drawn up by Consumers' Association to ensure consumers get a fair deal online and to provide them with protection if things go wrong.

Which? Web Traders agree to meet and abide by our Code of Practice (see 190–98). Complaints from consumers about the service from accepted Which? Web Traders will be investigated and permission to display the logo may be withdrawn. Consumers' Association believes that shopping online should be safe and the Which? Web Trader Scheme endeavours to set the standard for good practice on the Internet

When a UK company applies to Consumers' Association for permission to display this mark, that company must agree to keep to the code of practice and it must supply details and contact information. We then carry out checks to make sure the company is genuine. Once we have accepted it, we will carry out random checks to make sure they are keeping to the code.

If we receive reports that it is not keeping to our code, we will investigate and, if this is the case, we will ask the trader to put things right or remove that trader from the scheme. The process for making a complaint about a Which? Web Trader is detailed below. If a complaint comes from a Which? Online subscriber we will provide all necessary legal backup, if it is needed, using lawyers from the Which? Legal Service.

If you are not a Which? Online subscriber, you can still get help from Which? Legal Service.

If you are a Which? Online subscriber, you can also report your experiences – good and bad – in our Which? Online Web Trader Forum. If you are not a Which? Online subscriber but would like to report your experiences, send your comments to us by email (webtrader@which.net) and we will post them on to the Forum for you. If you would like us to follow anything up for you, or if you would like to provide information about a particular transaction, please include the order number or reference in your email.

Laws which apply to other forms of shopping also apply to online traders based in the UK. We will do our best, with your help and feedback, to make sure that the Which? Web Trader Code of Practice gives online shoppers the same level of confidence they enjoy elsewhere.

If you visit a web site with the Which? Web Trader logo which includes an auction section, please note that this part of the site is outside the remit of our Code of Practice. The law concerning auctions is different to the one applied to normal purchases (everyday transactions) and a consumer's statutory rights can be excluded. It is also likely that your purchase will be from a private individual, not the Which? Web Trader. We cannot ensure compliance by these individuals with our Code.

What is TrustUK?

TrustUK is the body set up to approve online codes of practice. Consumers' Association, the Alliance for Electronic Business and the Direct Marketing Association have worked together with support from the Department of Trade and Industry (DTI) in order to bring it about.

The purpose of TrustUK is to set a standard for the conduct of e-commerce between business and consumers. As e-commerce picks up, codes of practice may proliferate. These codes will vary in the types of things that they cover and in the level of protection that they provide. TrustUK will allow consumers to recognise whether the particular code which they are relying on does in fact meet its standards.

The criteria for TrustUK approval covers all the concerns that a consumer might have when deciding whether to shop online, for example, privacy or security.

The Which? Web Trader Code has been approved by TrustUK. The approval is granted by a Committee which is independent from the management of TrustUK.

Which? Web Trader Code of Practice

A trader displaying the Which? Web Trader logo on his or her web site agrees to follow these guidelines. It does NOT mean that Which? or any of its associate companies recommends the products the trader is offering or the customer service provided by the trader outside the areas covered in the Code.

Part 1: What the trader must do

The trader must provide clear and adequate information about his or her products and services to enable consumers to make informed decisions.

The trader's web site must include:

- The Which? Web Trader logo, incorporating the TrustUK logo. This must be displayed prominently on the web site so that consumers cannot miss it as they enter the site. The logo does not have to appear on the home page
- Full contact details, including phone and fax numbers, postal and email addresses and a contact for complaints
- The price of goods or services must be easily found and clearly shown in £'s. The trader must display the actual price the consumer will be charged without any hidden extras such as tax, packaging or delivery
- Clear ordering instructions

- A description of the different ways of paying
- A customer services phone number, the times when the service is available and the costs of the calls. Any customer service staff must be aware of the trader's obligations under the Code.
- The right to cancel the contract and how to exercise this right
- Any restrictions including how long the offer remains valid and any cooling-off periods
- An invitation to Which? Online customers to post comments about their experience of using traders' services on Which? Online forum discussions
- The terms and conditions of the trader's contract displayed clearly and plainly. They must be easily found on the site. The trader must state that the terms of the contract do not affect the consumer's statutory rights
- The trader must obtain the consent of customers to receive marketing email from the trader or from others.

Advertising

The trader's advertising must meet the standards of the British Codes of Advertising and Sales Promotion. In particular, it must be legal, decent, honest and truthful. It must also comply with the rulings of the ASA which you can see at **www.asa.org.uk**.

The trader should clearly identify any advertising on his or her site from the advertising of other people or organisations.

The trader must take care not to create a demand which cannot be met.

Returns and refunds

If the trader has a returns and refunds policy which gives consumers more rights than they have under the law or this code, he or she should inform the customer clearly, with easy-to-follow instructions.

Guarantees

If the trader is providing a guarantee or warranty, he or she must make the following clear:

- what is covered
- for how long
- that the guarantee or warranty is in addition to the consumers' statutory rights.

The Sale

1. Confirmation
Before the contract, the trader must confirm the price the consumer will pay.

After the contract, the trader must confirm the order by email or post, immediately after the order is placed. The confirmation must include:

- the name of the trader
- an order or reference number
- the total price to be paid by the consumer
- instructions on how to cancel the contract including to whom the cancellation notice may be sent and whether the customer must pay for the cost of returning the goods.

2. Cancellation
Unless the law permits otherwise, the trader must give consumers the right to cancel the contract within 7 working days without reason.

- In the case of goods, the 7 days start when the goods are received

- In the case of services, the 7 days start when the contract was made.

When the consumer cancels, the trader must return the payment within 30 days of the cancellation. The consumer may have to pay the cost of returning the goods.

3. Delivery
The trader must deliver the goods within 30 days, unless the consumer has agreed to a longer time. If the trader cannot deliver the goods within this time the consumer must be informed immediately and another time for delivery agreed upon. If another time cannot be agreed upon, the trader must offer the consumer a refund.

4. Receipts
The trader must provide the consumer with a receipt.

Mistakes, complaints and disputes

1. Consumer law
The trader must meet his or her obligations under the consumer protection laws currently in force.

2. Faulty goods
If the goods turn out to be faulty or different from those the consumer ordered, the trader must offer the consumer a full refund. The trader must give the refund as soon as possible and at the latest, within 30 days of agreeing to give the refund.

3. Mistakes in bills, receipts or payments
Any mistakes in bills, receipts or payments must be rectified as soon as possible, and at the latest within 30 days of agreeing to do so.

4. Complaints
The trader must have an effective system for handling complaints. The complaints procedure must be available online, easy to use and confidential. The trader must:

- acknowledge complaints within 5 working days
- advise the consumer how long it will take to resolve the complaint
- keep the consumer informed throughout the process.

5. Disputes
The trader must provide details about any dispute-solving scheme to which he or she belongs, including any Ombudsman scheme or regulator.

Privacy and security

1. Data Protection Act
The trader must meet the conditions of the Data Protection Act 1998 (DPA).

2. Privacy policy
The trader must have a privacy policy and implement it effectively. If the trader does not have one, the policy outlined below may be used and any changes made to suit the business.

The privacy policy must include the following:

- the trader must provide the consumer with the option to withhold personal information which is not needed for the transaction
- the trader must not collect sensitive personal information (see the Data Protection Act for definition) without the explicit consent of the consumer – for example, health or ethnic origin
- the trader must allow consumers easy access to their own personal information
- the trader must ensure that personal information is accurate and up to date
- the trader should hold personal information only for as long as it is needed for the purpose it was collected

- the trader must tell the consumer if he or she is going to transfer personal information outside the European Economic Area.

On the web site

The trader must provide the name of the person responsible for privacy matters.

The trader must display a clear and prominent statement before or at the time when the consumer provides personal information stating:

- what information is being collected
- how it is collected
- who is collecting the information
- what the information is to be used for
- if tracking technology is being used, such as cookies
- the trader will not send the consumer email without first obtaining his or her consent.

3. Security policy

The trader must have an effective security policy. It must be reviewed regularly.

This security policy must include the following:

- the trader must ensure that his or her web site is secure so that consumers' personal information and transactions remain confidential and cannot be interfered with
- the trader must ensure that the content of his or her site cannot be interfered with
- any subcontractors or third parties involved in the transaction must follow these principles and maintain a similar level of security
- the trader must take steps to protect Which? Web Trader and TrustUK logos against misuse.

On the web site

The trader must provide information about the type and level of security being used on his or her site and identify a person responsible for the security of that site. This person must:

- regularly review the security of the system
- make sure that any changes to the system are made in a secure way
- make sure that the trader follows the security guidelines of the system supplier.

Part 2: What the trader must not do

1. Unsolicited commercial email

The trader must not send untargeted mass-marketing emails to people with whom he or she has had no contact.

2. Children

Any communications aimed at children must be appropriate to their age and must not exploit their credulity, lack of experience or sense of loyalty.

The trader must not accept an order from someone he or she knows or suspects to be a child without the consent of the child's parent or carer.

If the child is under 12 years old, the trader must not collect any personal information without the consent of that child's parent or carer. If the child is over 12, the trader should collect only information necessary to send the child appropriate communications as long as the child understands what is involved.

The trader must not disclose information collected from children to anyone else without the consent of the child's parent or guardian.

The trader must not ask the child for personal information about other people. The trader must not entice the child to give personal information by offering a reward or a prize.

Part 3: What Which? will do

1. Legal advice

Subscribers to Which?Online who have problems after buying from a Web Trader will be entitled to free legal advice from Which? Legal Service. The trader must co-operate with Which? Legal Service to solve the problem.

2. Which? Web Trader Dispute Resolution Service

If the trader is unable to resolve a dispute with a consumer, the trader must inform the consumer that he or she may go to Which? Web Trader to have his or her complaint resolved. We will check to see whether the trader has handled the complaint properly and if appropriate, recommend a solution. Our decision will be binding on the trader but will not prevent the consumer from going to court.

Our independent service is free and available online to all consumers, no matter where they live. It is easy to use and quick, with clear time limits. We will file quarterly reports on its performance to TrustUK. If the consumer does not think that the complaint has been handled in accordance with these principles, he or she may refer it to TrustUK.

3. Monitoring

We will monitor the effectiveness of the Code through feedback, complaints, mystery shopping and other research. We will deliver a report to TrustUK concerning the compliance of the traders on the scheme.

4. Enforcement

If we discover that a trader has not complied with the Code, we will take enforcement action. We will investigate and, if appropriate, ask the trader to take action to resolve the problem. The trader must agree to take this action. If the breach is serious, the trader could be excluded from the scheme. There is an appeal procedure and we can provide details on request.

5. Review
The trader must be informed of major changes to the Code of Practice and will be given the opportunity to update his or her site accordingly.

Which? Web Traders

Accessories

1st Site	www.site-registrations.co.uk
Animail	www.animail.co.uk
Bookchair	www.bookchair.com
Brit Guides	www.britguides.com
Card Corporation	www.cardcorp.com
Carry Mug	www.carrymug.co.uk
Caseshop.com	www.caseshop.com
DataPet	www.datapet.co.uk
Fragrance Direct	www.fragrancedirect.co.uk/
FreeNumber Co	www.freenumber.freeserve.co.uk/
Genfair	www.genfair.com
Get1 Online	www.get1online.com
GHS Direct	www.ghs-direct.com/
Giltsharp	www.giltsharp.com/
Gospel Storehouse	www.gospelstorehouse.co.uk/
Grace Brown Interiors	www.gbinteriors.co.uk
iLearn.to	www.iLearn.to
JCB Works	www.jcbworks.com
Lawrights	www.lawrights.co.uk

For a complete and current list of Which? Web Traders go to
www.which.net/webtrader

ACCESSORIES

Left-Handed	www.left-handed.com
Lloyd & Jones	www.lloyd-jones.com
Mercian Labels	www.mercianlabels.co.uk
Mini Labels	www.minilabel.co.uk
Mjtech	www.mjtech.co.uk
Mortec	www.mortek.com/
Natural Friends	www.natural-friends.co.uk
Officepoint Fivestar	www.officepointfivestar.com
Onview.net	www.onview.net/onviewshop
Oxford School of Learning	www.osl-ltd.co.uk
Photogold	www.photogold.co.uk
R&J Howarth	www.thejewellers.net/
Skills Online	www.skills-online.net
Styleisland	www.styleisland.com/
The 0870 Co	www.the0870.co.uk
UKool	www.ukool.com
Urbanman	www.urbanman.co.uk
Worthaglance	www.worthaglance.com
X-Play	www.x-play.com

For a complete and current list of Which? Web Traders go to
www.which.net/webtrader

Auctions/Art

A'anside	www.aanside.co.uk
Antiques Directory	www.antiques-directory.co.uk
Card Inspirations	www.cardinspirations.co.uk
Clarice Cliff Co	www.claricecliff.co.uk
Clarice Cliff Collectors Store	www.claricecliff.com/shopping
Easyart	www.easyart.com
Essentially English	www.essentially-english.com
Fine Art Exposed	www.fineartexposed.com
Heaton Cooper Studio	www.heatoncooper.co.uk
In2Webs	www.i2w.co.uk
Ireland Exposed	www.irelandexposed.com
London Art	www.londonart.co.uk
Out of Afrika	www.outofafrika.co.uk
Pictures UK	www.pictures-uk.com
Race Art	www.raceart.co.uk
Redrobin	www.redrobin.co.uk
Simon Pym	www.pym-art.co.uk
Smart Craft	www.smartcraft.co.uk
Steve Bartrick	www.antiqueprints.com
Studio Arts	www.studioarts.co.uk
Sutcliffe Gallery	www.sutcliffe-gallery.co.uk/index.htm
The Artworks	www.the-artwork.co.uk
Visoni	www.visoni.com/

For a complete and current list of Which? Web Traders go to
www.which.net/webtrader

AUCTIONS/ART

Autos

Autoperfect	www.autoperfect.net/
Car Audio Direct	www.caraudiodirect.com
Caraudiodiscount	www.caraudiodiscount.com
Carbusters.com	www.carbusters.com
Carseekers	www.carseekers.co.uk
Coverallseatcovers	www.coverallseatcovers.com
Decibels	www.decibels.co.uk
Decibels	www.emark.co.uk
Find a Car Part	www.findacarpart.co.uk
Gomobile.co.uk	www.gomobileuk.co.uk
Holiday Autos	www.holidayautos.co.uk
Incar-Discount	www.incar-discount.co.uk
Incarepress	www.incarexpress.co.uk/
Mastercarsdirect	www.mastercarsdirect.com
OEM	www.oem-uk.com
Pure Research	www.pureresearch.co.uk
Sondel.co.uk	www.sondel.co.uk
Speeding Online	www.speeding.co.uk
Towing Brackets	www.towingbrackets.com/

AUTOS

For a complete and current list of Which? Web Traders go to
www.which.net/webtrader

Books and magazines

Alphabet Street	www.alphabetstreet.co.uk/
Antiques Directory	www.antiques-directory.co.uk
Audio Books	www.audiobooksatcrotchet.co.uk
Blackwell's Bookshops	www.bookshop.blackwell.co.uk
British Horse Society	www.britishhorse.com
Camdenlockbooks	www.camdenlockbooks.co.uk
Countryman Books	www.countryman.co.uk
Desktop Driving	www.desktopdriving.com/
Encyclopaedia Britannica International Ltd	www.britannica.co.uk
GBTour	www.gbtour.co.uk/
Good Book Guide	www.thegoodbookguide.com
Gospel Storehouse	www.gospelstorehouse.co.uk/
Infront Ltd	www.infront.co.uk
Internet Talking Bookshop	www.orma.co.uk
Kingdon Faith	www.kingdomfaith.com
Manchester University Press	www.manchesteruniversity press.co.uk/
Ottaker's PLC	www.ottakars.co.uk
PC BookShops	www.pcbooks.co.uk
Pickabook	www.pickabook.co.uk
Red Onion Books	www.redonionbooks.com
Saxons	www.saxons.co.uk
Schofield and Sims	www.schofieldandsims.co.uk

BOOKS & MAGAZINES

For a complete and current list of Which? Web Traders go to
www.which.net/webtrader

Scottish-Roots	www.scottish-roots.co.uk
Society of Genealogists	www.sog.org/bookshop.html
Student Bookworld	www.Studentbookworld.com/
Study-Books	www.study-books.com
Teacher Trading	www.teachertrading.co.uk/
The BBC Shop	www.bbcshop.com
The Country Bookstore	www.countrybookstore.co.uk
The Magazine Shop	www.magazineshop.co.uk

Computing

1st Domains	www.1stdomains.co.uk
1st Domains	www.ac-communications.co.uk/
A One	www.aone.co.uk
A2Zcomputerproducts	www.a2zcomputerproducts.com
acelogic	www.acelogic.com/
Addax	www.addax.co.uk
Appleby Solutions	www.appleby-solutions.com/
A-Q	www.a-q.co.uk
Axon Computers	www.axon.ltd.uk
Beaufortweb	www.beaufortweb.co.uk
Big Rom	www.bigrom.co.uk
Cablefind	www.cablefind.com

For a complete and current list of Which? Web Traders go to
www.which.net/webtrader

Calibre Computing	www.calibrecomputing.net
Cartridge Co.	www.cartridgeco.co.uk
Cartridge Shop	www.cartridgeshop.co.uk
CCT Global	www.cctglobal.com/
CD Imports	www.cdimports.com
Chips	www.chipsworld.co.uk
City 2000	www.city2000.com
CNRL	www.chrisnaylor.co.uk
consumables.net	www.consumables.net/
Data Developments	www.data-developments.co.uk
Directintel	www.directintel.com
Distributor Systems International	www.dsiweb.co.uk
Domain Name Shop	www.domainnameshop.co.uk/
EntWeb	www.entweb.co.uk
Evesham Micros Ltd	www.evesham.com
ExtraLAN Ltd	www.extralan.com/
Frugal Names	www.frugalnames.com/
Get Networking	www.getnetworking.net
glidescope	www.glideslopesoftware.co.uk
GT Office Equipment	www.gtoffice.co.uk
Home PC Supplies	www.rpcs.co.uk/
HUBNUT	www.hubnut.net/
Ink and Stuff	www.inkandstuff.co.uk
ink4u.co.uk	www.ink4u.co.uk/

COMPUTING

For a complete and current list of Which? Web Traders go to
www.which.net/webtrader

The Which? Guide to Shopping on the Internet

Ink-net	www.itosn.com/which
Integrex	www.integrex.co.uk
Internetters	www.internetters.co.uk
IRL.COM	www.irl.com/
justflight	www.justflight.com
Learning Store	www.learningstore.co.uk
Name Your Price	www.nameyourprice.co.uk
Name2.net	www.name2.net
Neotogo	www.neotogo.com/
Net2	www.net2.co.uk
NetShop	www.netshop.co.uk
NJH Consultants	www.njh-consultants.com/
Novatech	www.novatech.co.uk
NS Design	www.nsdesign.co.uk
Pacer Graphics	www.pacer-graphics.co.uk
PC Assist	www.pcassist.co.uk
PCUpgrader	www.pcupgrader.co.uk/
PDA	www.pdacentre.com
Pick a Web	www.pickaweb.co.uk/
Purple Beaver	www.purplebeaver.net
Quiet PC	www.quietpc.com/
RamJam Web Hosting	www.ramjam.net
Raxco	www.raxco.co.uk
Redspan	www.redspan.com/
Scotgold	www.scotgold.com

For a complete and current list of Which? Web Traders go to
www.which.net/webtrader

COMPUTING

Shop!	www.shop-tv.co.uk
ShopInk	www.shopink.co.uk
ShoutLoud	www.shoutloud.com
Simply Computers	www.simply.co.uk
Smart Domains	www.smartdomains.co.uk
Software Paradise	www.softwareparadise.co.uk
Source	www.source.uk.com/
Sterling Inkjet	www.sterling-inkjet.co.uk
Stuart Manufacturing	www.smco.co.uk
Tape City	www.tapecity.co.uk/
Target Media	www.targetmedia.co.uk
The 0870 Co	www.the0870.co.uk
The Ink Factory	www.theinkfactory.co.uk/
The Potty Price Shop	www.thepottypriceshop.co.uk /
Tonik	www.tonik.co.uk
Touchstone UK	www.touchstoneuk.com/
TUSE Ltd	www.theurlstockexchange.com
UK Domains	www.ukdomains.net
Unwired	www.unwired.co.uk
URWired.com	www.urwired.com
Webxone	www.webxone.com
Your Name Here	www.your-name-here.co.uk
Zarr.com	www.zarr.com/answers/

COMPUTING

For a complete and current list of Which? Web Traders go to
www.which.net/webtrader

Department stores

1 Shop for All	www.1shopforall.co.uk
Adventure Shop	www.adventureshop.co.uk
AJM Shopping	www.ajmshopping.co.uk/
barclaysquare	www.barclaysquare.co.uk
Easyshop	www.easyshop.co.uk
Gourmet Cookware Co.	www.gourmetcook.co.uk/
Infront Ltd	www.infront.co.uk
Jungle.com	www.jungle.com
Netline	www.netline.co.uk
Pupsnuts	www.pupsnuts.com
QVC	www.qvcuk.com
Shop!	www.shop-tv.co.uk
Shoppersempire	www.shoppersempire.com
Taverymuch	www.taverymuch.com/
ToyBoy	www.thetoyboy.com
World of Shopping	www.worldofshopping.com

Electronics and cameras

1st Cameras	www.1stcameras.com
247 Cellphone	www.247cellphone.com
A1 Communications	www.a1comms.co.uk
Adventure Shop	www.adventureshop.co.uk
Appliance Online	www.applianceonline.co.uk

For a complete and current list of Which? Web Traders go to
www.which.net/webtrader

Axex	www.axex.co.uk
Ben Evans & Son	www.bedirect.co.uk
BestStuff	www.beststuff.co.uk
Call Crazy	www.callcrazy.com/
Camera Corner	www.cameracorner.co.uk
Cameras Direct	www.camerasdirect.co.uk
Capital Sound & Vision	www.unbeatable.co.uk
CD-Writer.com	www.cd-writer.com/
Cellect	www.cellect.co.uk
Cheap-Mobiles	www.cheap-mobiles.com
comet	www.comet.co.uk
Complete Comms	www.completecomms.co.uk/
Custome Mobiles	www.custommobile.com
Cyrane Limited (Value Direct)	www.value-direct.co.uk
Digital Choice	www.digitalchoice.co.uk
Domestics2u	www.domestics2u.co.uk
EDUK	www.electricaldiscountuk.co.uk
Electric Savers	www.electricsavers.co.uk
Electrical Direct	www.electricaldirect.co.uk
electricalestore	www.electrical.coop.co.uk/
Electronic Machines Corporation	www.e-machine.co.uk
Empire Direct	www.empiredirect.co.uk
ETC Communications	www.etccomms.co.uk

ELECTRONICS & CAMERAS

For a complete and current list of Which? Web Traders go to
www.which.net/webtrader

ELECTRONICS & CAMERAS

FreedomPhones	www.freedomphones.co.uk
Freeline Comms Ltd	www.freeline.co.uk
Freenet Electrical	www.freenet.ltd.uk
hazelnet	www.hazelnet.co.uk
HiFiBitZ	www.hifibitz.co.uk
Hifistereo	www.hifi-stereo.com/
Home Electrical Direct	www.hed.co.uk
Hutchisons	www.hutchisons.co.uk/
HW Audio	www.hwaudio.co.uk/
Ifone	www.ifone.co.uk
Internet Cameras Direct	www.internetcamerasdirect.co.uk
Ist Trip Camera	www.1tripcamera.com/
Jessops	www.jessops.com
Jonathan Harris	www.jonathanharris.co.uk
Justphones	www.justphones.co.uk/
Kamera Direct	www.bestcameras.co.uk/
L8Shop	www.L8Shop.co.uk
Let's Automate	www.letsautomate.com/
Lowcost Computers	www.lowcost-computers.co.uk
Mailshots	www.mailshots.co.uk
Mail UK Ltd	www.mailuk.com
Megapixels	www.megapixels.com/
Miah Telecom	www.miah-telecom.co.uk/
Miller Bros	www.millerbros.co.uk
Mjtech	www.mjtech.com/

For a complete and current list of Which? Web Traders go to
www.which.net/webtrader

Mobile Tones	www.mobiletones.com/
Mobile Zone	www.mobilezone.co.uk
Mobileshop	www.mobileshop.com
My Nokia	www.my-nokia.co.uk/
O'gorman's	www.ogormans.co.uk
Optimair	www.optimair.co.uk
Phoneshop Online	www.phoneshop.uk.com
PhotograhicDirect	www.photographicdirect.co.uk
Prime 2000	www.prime2000.co.uk
Purley Radio	www.purleyradio.co.uk
R-P-R.co.uk	www.r-p-r.co.uk/
RTD	www.rtd.uk.com
Sherwoods	www.sherwoods-photo.com
Shop!	www.shop-tv.co.uk
Simply Radios	www.simplyradios.com
Small Talk Communications	www.smalltalk.co.uk
Source	www.source.uk.com/
talkmobiles	www.talkmobiles.co.uk
Teletronics	www.teletronics.co.uk/
Tempo Electrical	www.tempo.co.uk
The Carphone Warehouse	www.carphonewarehouse.com
Time2Talk	www.time2talk.co.uk/
Toade.com	www.toade.com/
Trident UK	www.tridentonline.co.uk
Ukappliances.co.uk	www.ukappliances.co.uk/

ELECTRONICS & CAMERAS

For a complete and current list of Which? Web Traders go to
www.which.net/webtrader

Urbanman	www.urbanman.co.uk
VC Direct	www.vacuumcleanersdirect.com
Virtual Electrical	www.v-e.co.uk
Webelectricals	www.webelectricals.co.uk
We-Sell-It	www.we-sell-it.co.uk
Whitebox	www.whitebox.co.uk/

Entertainment

Aloud.com	www.aloud.com
atlantistickets	www.atlantistickets.co.uk/
Bensons World of Home Entertainment	www.bensonsworld.co.uk
Blackstar	www.blackstar.co.uk
Britannica	www.britannica.co.uk
Choicesdirect	www.choicesdirect.co.uk/
Disks2go	www.disks2go.co.uk
DVD Street	www.dvdstreet.co.uk
Epic Heroes	www.epicheroes.com
Gameland	www.gameland.co.uk
Games Street	www.gamesstreet.co.uk/
Games Terminal	www.gamesterminal.com
Inter DVD	www.interdvd.co.uk
Kingcat.co.uk	www.kingcat.co.uk
Mania Entertainment	www.mania.co.uk
Moviemail	www.moviem.co.uk

For a complete and current list of Which? Web Traders go to
www.which.net/webtrader

Neotogo	www.neotogo.com/
Nextgen	www.next-gen.co.uk
Night Café	www.nightcafe.co.uk
Out-of-the-ordinary.com	www.out-of-the-ordinary.com
Petit Bout	www.petitbout.co.uk/
Predict	www.predict.co.uk
The Fish Consultancy	www.gamesandvideos.com
The Party Store	www.thepartystore.co.uk
The Video Shop	www.videoshop.co.uk
UK DVD Rental	www.ukdvdrentals.co.uk

Fashion

4xl	www.forxl.co.uk
Abooga.Com	www.abooga.com
absolutelyme	www.absolutelyme.com
Acorn Printing	www.acorn-printing.co.uk
Affordable Designers	www.affordabledesigners.co.uk
Affordable Sunglasses	www.affordablesunglasses.co.uk/
Argenteus	www.argenteus.co.uk
Bags of Time	www.bagsoftime.co.uk
Bare Essentials	www.bareessentials.uk.com/
Beachwear.net	www.beachwear.net
Bella Lingerie	www.lingerie-uk.officeuk.com
Bluebelle.co.uk	www.bluebelle.co.uk/
Blush Lingerie	www.blushlingerie.co.uk/

For a complete and current list of Which? Web Traders go to www.which.net/webtrader

Cafe Coton	www.cafecoton.co.uk
ccbparis	www.ccb-paris.com/
CleverPants	www.cleverpants.com
Cloggs of Oasis	www.cloggs.co.uk/
Clothingtrends.co.uk	www.clothingtrends.co.uk/
Cool Diamonds	www.cooldiamonds.com
Creative Watch	www.creativewatch.co.uk/
Designer Deals Direct	www.designerdealsdirect.com
Discount Sports	www.discountsports.co.uk
Double-D.com	www.double-d.com
Easyshop	www.easyshop.co.uk
Ecuffs	www.ecuffs.com
Ecuffs	www.eshopone.co.uk
Elingerie.uk.net	www.elingerie.uk.net/
Erotinet	www.erotinet.co.uk/
Fade fashion	www.fade-fashion.com
Fingzfashions	www.fingzfashions.com
Gatefish	www.gatefish.com
Gentleman's Shop	www.gentlemans-shop.co.uk
Gold Factory Online	www.goldfactory.co.uk
Gordon Stoker and Sons	www.gordonstoker.co.uk/
Hector Russell Kiltmaker	www.hector-russell.com
Ice Cool	www.icecool.co.uk
Ireland's Gold	www.irelandsgold.com
JCB Works	www.jcbworks.com

For a complete and current list of Which? Web Traders go to
www.which.net/webtrader

FASHION

Jewellery Catalogue	www.thejewellerycatalogue.co.uk/
Jewellery Warehouse	www.jewellerywarehouse.co.uk
Jewellery2000	www.jewellery2000.com
Joe Browns	www.joebrowns.co.uk
Joycetreasure	www.joycetreasure.co.uk
Just Sloggi	www.justsloggi.co.uk
Knicker Locker	www.knickerlocker.com
Ladybwear	www.ladybwear.com
Legs Express	www.legsexpress.co.uk/
Lionel Jacobs	www.lioneljacobs.co.uk/
Lornas-Lingerie	www.lornas-lingerie.com
Madhouse	www.madhouse.co.uk/
Marcus Shoes	www.marcusshoes.com
Midnight Express	www.midnightexpress.co.uk
Natives	www.natives.co.uk
Netslug	www.netslug.com
No time to browse	www.notimetobrowse.co.uk
Pediwear	www.pediwear.co.uk
R P Collections	www.rdsweb.co.uk/nilenew
Regalo's	www.linedancing.co.uk
Regent Street Mall	www.regentstreetmall.com
Retrospecs	www.retrospecs.co.uk
Say It With Jewels	www.sayitwithjewels.com
Select Online	www.select.uk.co
Sexyshoes	www.sexyfootwear.co.uk

FASHION

For a complete and current list of Which? Web Traders go to
www.which.net/webtrader

FASHION

Shirt Press	www.shirt-press.co.uk
Shoe Shop	www.shoe-shop.com
Shoes Direct	www.shoesdirect.co.uk
Shop Gold	www.shopgold.co.uk/
Shop!	www.shop-tv.co.uk
Silk Stockings	www.silkstockings.co.uk
Silverene.com	www.www.silverene.com/
Sizedwell	www.sizedwell.co.uk
Snickers Workwear	www.snickersworkwear.co.uk
Sovereign Diamonds	www.sovereigndiamonds.com
Sportsbras	www.sportsbras.co.uk
Sportsmart	www.sportsmart.co.uk
Sportswearhouse	www.sportswearhouse.co.uk
Stafford-And-Brown	www.stafford-and-brown.com
Street Urchins	www.streeturchins.com/
Sumina	www.sumina.co.uk
Swatch Heaven	www.topbrands.net
Sweet Sensations	www.sweetsensations-int.com
The Tie Company	www.thetiecompany.co.uk
TieNet	www.tienet.co.uk
Ultimate Shoes	www.ultimate-shoes.com
Urbanman	www.urbanman.co.uk
Usisi	www.usisidirect.com
Wear4.com	www.wear4.com/
Zercon.com Ltd	www.zercon.com

For a complete and current list of Which? Web Traders go to
www.which.net/webtrader

Finance and property

Alder Broker Group Ltd	www.abgltd.co.uk
Boatinsure	www.boatinsure.co.uk
CIPFA	www.cipfa.org.uk/publications
Direct Line	www.directline.com
Direct Travel	www.direct-travel.co.uk/
Elitemortgages	www.elitemortgages.co.uk
Etax Limited	www.etax.co.uk
Flat-Sharer.com	www.flat-sharer.com/
Froglet.com	www.froglet.com/
Grovewood Financial Management	www.gfm-ifa.co.uk/
Insurance Shopper	www.insuranceshopperonline.com
Insurance UK	www.insurance.uk.com/
Jackson Insurance Services	www.jacksonsinsure.co.uk
LMN8	www.lmn8.com
Money Mate	www.moneymate.co.uk
NIS	www.nis.ndirect.co.uk
Policy Direct	www.policydirect.co.uk/
Rapid Insure	www.rapidinsure.co.uk/
ROK Associates Credit/Debt Management Limited	www.ctoc.co.uk
ScotWills	www.scotwills.co.uk
studentwatchout	www.studentwatchout.co.uk/
Wise Money	www.wisemoney.com
Wisebuy Publications	www.wisebuy.co.uk

For a complete and current list of Which? Web Traders go to
www.which.net/webtrader

FINANCE & PROPERTY

Flowers and gifts

101Gifts	www.101gifts.co.uk
A'anside	www.4-a-song.com
A'anside	www.aanside.co.uk
Aardvarkstore.com	www.aardvarkstore.com/
Abooga.Com	www.abooga.com
Adventure Shop	www.adventureshop.co.uk
All Things Cornish	www.allthingscornish.com
Alternative Gift Co.	www.alt-gifts.com
Battersea Pen Home	www.penhome.co.uk
BelphilLondon Cigars	www.belphillondoncigars.com/
Buckie Bears	www.buckiebears.mcmail.com/
Buckingham Gate	www.buckinghamgate.com
Business Toys	www.businesstoys.co.uk/
Buy Appointment	www.buy-appointment.co.uk
Canalshop	www.canalshop.co.uk
Card Inspirations	www.cardinspirations.co.uk
Card-box	www.card-box.co.uk
Champers Direct	www.champersdirect.co.uk
Charity Cards	www.charitycards.co.uk
Charlie Crow Costumes	www.charliecrow.com/
Chiasmus	www.chiasmus.co.uk
Clare Florist	www.clareflorist.com
Click the Cookie	www.clickthecookie.co.uk/

For a complete and current list of Which? Web Traders go to
www.which.net/webtrader

Company of Bears	www.companyofbears.com
Crystal Cavern	www.crystalcavern.com/
Direct Cards	www.directcards.com/
Direct Watch	www.directwatch.com
Discovery	www.discovery-gifts.co.uk
Dont know What to Buy	www.dontknowwhattobuy.com/
Emporium	www.emporiumuk.com/
Endlessfun	www.endlessfun.com
Eshopone	www.eshopone.co.uk
Essentially English	www.essentially-english.com
Fiorito	www.fiorito.co.uk/cgi-bin/ Fiorito.storefront/home
First Flowers	www.firstflowers.com
Fizzynet	www.malltraders.com/fizzynet
Flowergram	www.flowergram.co.uk
Flowers Direct	www.flowersdirect.co.uk/
Flowers2send	www.flowers2send.com/
Freesia.co.uk	www.freesia.co.uk/
GasgdetNet!	www.gadgetnet.co.uk
giftinspiration.com	www.giftinspiration.com
Gifts and gadgets	www.giftsandgadgets.co.uk
Giftsforbirds	www.giftsforbirds.com
giftwarren.com	www.giftwarren.com/
Hot Box	www.hotbox.co.uk
Hugs and Cuddles	www.hugsandcuddles.co.uk

FLOWERS & GIFTS

For a complete and current list of Which? Web Traders go to
www.which.net/webtrader

FLOWERS & GIFTS

Interflora	www.interflora.co.uk
Internet Gift Store	www.internetgiftstore.com
Interteddy	www.interteddy.com
J&M Giftware	www.jandmgiftware.co.uk
K2Man	www.k2man.co.uk
Kandles & Co.	www.kandles.co.uk
Kitsch	www.kitsch.co.uk/
Knopfler CDs	www.knopfler.com
Lockwoods Florists	www.lockwoodsflorists.co.uk
Made-in-Sheffield	www.made-in-sheffield.com/
Malkin Clocks	www.malkinclocks.co.uk
Manners Mail Order	www.mannersmailorder.co.uk
Navy News	www.navynews.co.uk/index.htm
Need a Present	www.needapresent.co.uk
Netfysh	www.netfysh.com
Nottingham Lace	www.nottingham-lace.co.uk
Occassions Observed	www.ocob.co.uk
Otherland Toys	www.otherlandtoys.co.uk
Out of Afrika	www.outofafrika.co.uk
Party Domain	www.partydomain.co.uk
Perfectly Priced Perfumes	www.perfectlypricedperfumes.co.uk
Portwaycollection	www.portwaycollection.co.uk
Presents Direct	www.presentsdirect.com/
Pupsnuts	www.pupsnuts.com
Pure Research	www.pureresearch.co.uk

For a complete and current list of Which? Web Traders go to
www.which.net/webtrader

Red Ribbon Gifts	www.redribbongifts.co.uk
Remember When	www.remember-when.co.uk
RichWorld	www.richworld.co.uk
Ruana	www.ruana.net
Say It With Jewels	www.sayitwithjewels.com
Scottish Crafts Direct	www.scottishcraftsdirect.com
ShopScotland	www.shopscotland.net
Silly Jokes	www.SillyJokes.co.uk/
Simply Thankyou	www.simplythankyou.co.uk
Snapcards	www.snapcards.co.uk
Something Special UK	www.somethingspecialuk.com/
Stuck for a Gift	www.stuckforagift.com
Teleflorist	www.teleflorist.co.uk
The Cap Factory	www.thecapfactory.co.uk/asp/partners.asp
The Cottage Garden Flower Shop	www.cgfs.co.uk
The Owl Barn	www.the-owl-barn.com
The Stationery Store	www.stationerystore.co.uk/
Things to engrave	www.thingstoengrave.co.uk/
Tree Gifts	www.treegifts.com/
Urbanman	www.urbanman.co.uk
Wheesh.com	www.wheesh.com/
World Tree	www.worldtree.org

FLOWERS & GIFTS

For a complete and current list of Which? Web Traders go to
www.which.net/webtrader

Food and drink

800 Hampers	www.800hampers.com/
AleStore	www.alestore.co.uk/
Amivin	www.amivin.com
Art Of Brewing	www.art-of-brewing.co.uk
Berry Bros & Rudd	www.bbr.co.uk
Bluemango	www.bluemango.co.uk
Brownes Chocolates	www.brownes.co.uk
Buy Wine Online	www.buywineonline.co.uk
Carrie-Janes	www.carrie-janes.co.uk
Chilli Willie's Spices by Post	www.chilli-willie.co.uk
Chocolatier	www.chocolatier-electro.com
Clearwater Hampers	www.hamper.com
Cole's Traditional Foods	www.colestrad.co.uk
Cucina Direct	www.cucinadirect.co.uk
Cyber Candy	www.cybercandy.co.uk
Drink 2 Drink	www.drink2drink.co.uk
Drink and Stuff	www.drinkstuff.com
Drinx	www.drinx.com
E. Botham & Sons Ltd	www.botham.co.uk
eAbsinthe	www.eabsinthe.com
Eshopone	www.eshopone.co.uk
French Hampers	www.FrenchHampers.com/
Getoily	www.getoily.com/

FOOD & DRINK

For a complete and current list of Which? Web Traders go to
www.which.net/webtrader

Gifttodrink	www.gifttodrink.co.uk
Glenfiddich	www.glenfiddich.com
Gourmet 2000	www.gourmet2000.co.uk
Gourmet World	www.gourmet-world.co.uk
Grey's Teas	www.greysteas.co.uk
Hebrideancottage	www.hebrideancottage.co.uk
Iceland Frozen Foods Plc	www.icelandfreeshop.com
Iorganic	www.iorganic.co.uk
La Boheme	www.laboheme.uk.com
Laymont and Shaw	www.laymont-shaw.co.uk
Martin's Seafresh	www.martins-seafresh.co.uk
Mckean	www.mckean.co.uk
Mount Fuji	www.mountfuji.co.uk/
Now365	www.now365.co.uk/
Offlicencedirect	www.offlicencedirect.com/
Olives et al	www.olivesetal.co.uk
Organic Oxygen	www.organic-oxygen.co.uk
Present Taste Ltd	www.chocolatestore.com
Provender Delicatessen	www.provender.co.uk
Pure Wine	www.purewine.co.uk/
Qualitymeat2u	www.qualitymeat2u.com/
River Valley Wine	www.rivervalleywine.com
Scottish Smoked Salmon	www.smokedsalmon.uk.com
Shetland Seafood	www.shetlandseafood.co.uk/
Susman's Biltong	www.susman.com

FOOD & DRINK

For a complete and current list of Which? Web Traders go to
www.which.net/webtrader

Take It from Here	www.tifh.co.uk
Tasteofengland	www.tasteofengland.co.uk
The Coffee Tree Company	www.coffee-tree.co.uk
The Fish Society	www.thefishsociety.co.uk
The Olive Grove Ltd	www.olives.uk.com
Vinitalia	www.vinitalia.com

Health and beauty

absolutelyme	www.absolutelyme.com
Bigboy Condoms	www.bigboycondoms.co.uk/
Birminghams	www.pharmacyperfumery.com
Blademail	www.blademail.co.uk/
Blushingbuyer	www.blushingbuyer.co.uk
Burgins Perfumery	www.burginsperfumery.co.uk/
ccbparis	www.ccb-paris.com/
Denise Brown	www.denisebrown.co.uk
Disability Supplies	www.disabilitysupplies.com/
Fragrance Direct	www.fragrancedirect.co.uk/
Grooming4Men	www.grooming4men.com/
haircare4Men	www.haircare4men.com/
Hairstyling	www.hairstyling.co.uk/
HerbalNet	www.herbalnet.co.uk
Holistic Hands	www.holistichands.co.uk/
HQhair	www.hqhair.com/

For a complete and current list of Which? Web Traders go to
www.which.net/webtrader

Internet Condoms	www.internetcondoms.com
Lookfantastic.com Ltd	www.lookfantastic.com
Martha Hill	www.marthahill.com
Menses	www.menses.co.uk
MySkinCare	www.myskincare.co.uk
Natural Friends	www.natural-friends.co.uk
Neutral Health	www.neutralheath.co.uk/
NHR Organic Oils	www.nhr.kz
ovs.net	www.ovs.net
Pitrok	www.pitrok.co.uk
Posture Point	www.posture.co.uk
Priceright	www.priceright.co.uk
Sportabac	www.sportabac.co.uk
United Condoms	www.unitedcondoms.com/

Home and garden

Appliance world	www.applianceworld.org.uk
Aquatics Online	www.aquatics-online.co.uk/
Ashbourne Linen	www.ashbournelinen.co.uk
Bearwalls	www.sterne.u-net.com/bearwalls/index.htm
Bernards	www.bernards.co.uk/
Bluepet	www.bluepet.co.uk/
Bouchon	www.bouchon.co.uk/
Bouldercraft	www.bouldercraft.com/
Candle Room	www.thecandleroom.co.uk

HOME & GARDEN

For a complete and current list of Which? Web Traders go to
www.which.net/webtrader

Cane Furniture Online	www.canefurniture-online.co.uk
Capital Gardens	www.capital-gardens.co.uk
Caseshop.com	www.caseshop.com
Chandeliers.co.uk	www.chandeliers.com/
Clarice Cliff Co	www.claricecliff.co.uk
CMS Gardens	www.cmsgardens.co.uk
Culliners Catering Equipment	www.culliners.co.uk
D&R Supplies	www.tool-signshop.co.uk
Danish House	www.triptrap.co.uk
Deco Deli	www.decodeli.com/
Direct Gardens	www.direct-gardens.com
Direct Sales	www.directsales.org.uk
Discounted Heating	www.discountedheating.co.uk
Diy Ltd	www.diy.ltd.uk
Diypcs	www.diypcs.co.uk/
Doors Direct	www.doorsdirect.co.uk
Dr Growgood	www.drgrowgood.co.uk
Dryden Aqua	www.1x1x1.co.uk
Eastleigh Services	www.eastleigh-services.co.uk
Easy Gardens	www.easygardens.net
Easy Warehouse	www.easywarehouse.co.uk/
Edkins Aquatics	www.equatics.co.uk/
E-Garden	www.e-garden.co.uk/
electricalestore	www.electrical.coop.co.uk/
Elegant Clocks	www.elegantclocks.co.uk

For a complete and current list of Which? Web Traders go to
www.which.net/webtrader

Envirocareonline.co.uk	www.envirocareonline.co.uk
Eshopone	www.eshopone.co.uk
Essentially English	www.essentially-english.com
Essex Appliances	www.essex-appliances.co.uk
Euroffice	www.euroffice.co.uk
Express Cleaning Supplies	www.express-cleaning-supplies.co.uk
Extensive	www.extensive.co.uk
Foundation Building	www.foundationbuilding.com
Fox DIY	www.foxdiy.com
Furniture Busters	www.furniturebusters.com/
Furniture Webstore	www.furniturewebstore.co.uk
G E Tools	www.getools.co.uk/
GardenMachinery.com	www.gardenmachinery.com
Gardenmachines	www.gardenmachines.com
Gas Fire Sales	www.gasfiresales.co.uk
Gas flame heating co	www.fires-direct.co.uk
Global Power	www.globalpower.co.uk
Gone Gardening	www.gonegardening.com/
Goodasitlooks	www.goodasitlooks.com
Handytools	www.handytools.co.uk
Head Start Pets	htt://www.headstartpets.co.uk/
In-Sinks	www.kitchen-sinks.co.uk
Integratedkitchenappliances	www.integrated kitchenappliances.co.uk

HOME & GARDEN

For a complete and current list of Which? Web Traders go to
www.which.net/webtrader

HOME & GARDEN

Its Great Shopping	www.itsgreatshopping.co.uk/
Itslondon	www.itslondon.co.uk/
Langdon	www.langardirect.com
Leighton Buzzard Garden Centre	www.gardengifts.co.uk
Lock Centre Group	www.lockcentre.com
Lockshop-Warehouse	www.lockshop-warehouse.co.uk/
London Art	www.londonart.co.uk
Maelstrom	www.maelstrom.co.uk
Malkin Clocks	www.malkinclocks.co.uk
Manners Mail Order	www.mannersmailorder.co.uk
Mearns Craft	www.mearnscraft.co.uk
Mobel Designs	www.sliding-door-wardrobes.co.uk
MowDIRECT	www.mowdirect.co.uk
Mower World	www.mowerworld.co.uk/
Mowers Online	www.mowers-online.co.uk
Mythology Rugs	www.mythology-rugs.com/
Netpine.co.uk	www.netpine.co.uk
Nicky's Nursery	www.nickys-nursery.co.uk
Out of Afrika	www.outofafrika.co.uk
partell.co.uk	www.partell.co.uk/
Pet Company	www.petcompany.co.uk/
Pet Medical Centre	www.petmc.co.uk
PetPlanet	www.petplanet.co.uk
Plumb World	www.plumbworld.co.uk

For a complete and current list of Which? Web Traders go to
www.which.net/webtrader

PoolStore	www.poolstore.co.uk
Pots and Pans	www.pots-and-pans.co.uk/
Priceright	www.priceright.co.uk
Prime 2000	www.prime2000.co.uk
Primrose Kitchens	www.primrose.co.uk
Pyramid Europe Ltd	www.solosite.net/pyramid/
Quality Electrical Direct	www.qed-uk.com
Quote Checkers	www.quotecheckers.co.uk
Ridgequest	www.ridgequest.co.uk
Robert Dyas	www.robertdyasdirect.co.uk
Roots Kitchens	www.rootskitchens.co.uk
Ruana	www.ruana.net
Rugs and Stuff	www.rugsandstuff.co.uk/
Ru-lefthanded	www.ru-lefthanded.co.uk/
Salvoweb	www.salvoweb.com/
Scales Express	www.scalesexpress.com/
Seating VFM	www.seatingvfm.com
Shop!	www.shop-tv.co.uk
Showerail	www.showerail.co.uk/
Space2	www.space2.com
The Garden Supply Company	www.gardensupply.co.uk
The Mexican Hammock Company	www.hammocks.co.uk
The Plant Directory	www.the-plant-directory.com /
The Tin Pot	www.thetinpot.co.uk/

HOME & GARDEN

For a complete and current list of Which? Web Traders go to
www.which.net/webtrader

Theshakerworkshop	www.theshakerworkshop.co.uk
Thomas Crapper	www.thomas-crapper.com/
ToolFast	www.toolfast.co.uk
ToolPost	www.toolpost.co.uk
Tools Direct	www.terratruck.co.uk
Wallpaper Online	www.wallpaperonline.co.uk
Wheredidyoubuythat	www.wheredidyoubuythat.com
Workallhours.com	www.workallhours.com

Music

101	www.101cd.com
Abbey Records	www.abbeyrecords.com
Amazon	www.amazon.co.uk
Applesound	www.applesound.co.uk
Audio Street	www.audiostreet.co.uk/
axemail.com	www.axemail.com/
Axis Music	www.onlinemusicshop.co.uk
BURBs	www.burbs.co.uk
CD Selections	www.cdselections.com
Chamberlain	www.chamberlainmusic.com
Crotchet	www.crotchet.co.uk
Dalriada	www.argyllweb.com/dalriada
Dancetime	www.dancetime.co.uk
Dawson's Music	www.dawsons.co.uk
Disc-n-tape	www.disc-n-tape.co.uk

For a complete and current list of Which? Web Traders go to
www.which.net/webtrader

DJ Shop-UK	www.djshop-uk.com/
Drum Ltd	www.drumltd.com
Highly Strung	www.highlystrung.co.uk/
Is this music	www.isthismusic.com/
Kids Cds and Tapes	www.kidscdsandtapes.com
Kingdom Faith	www.kingdomfaith.com
Knopfler CDs	www.knopfler.com
Look Music	www.lookmusic.com
Music In Scotland	www.musicinscotland.com
MusicScotland	www.musicscotland.com/
Nervous Records	www.nervous.co.uk
Night Café	www.nightcafe.co.uk
PieDog	www.piedog.com
Recollections	www.recollections.co.uk
Regent Guitars	www.regentguitars.co.uk/ frontpage.htm
Ruana	www.ruana.net
Seaford Music	www.seaford-music.co.uk
Sounds Live	www.soundslive.co.uk
Soundsvisual.co.uk	www.soundsvisual.co.uk/
The Bebop Shop	www.thebebopshop.com
The Music Index	www.themusicindex.com
Total Home Entertainment	www.4-a-song.com
West Pacific Music	www.westpacificmusic.com
XMPDVD	www.xmpdvd.co.uk/

M U S I C

For a complete and current list of Which? Web Traders go to
www.which.net/webtrader

Sports and hobbies

4 Mil Models	www.4milmodels.com/
Adventure Shop	www.adventureshop.co.uk
Albany Hill	www.albanyhill.com
Asksport	www.asksport.com
Balls Fore Golf	www.balls-fore-golf.co.uk
Bicyclenet.co.uk	www.bicyclenet.co.uk
Boat Paint	www.boatpaint.co.uk
Boat-net	www.boat-net.co.uk
British Collectible Cards	www.psi-soft.co.uk
Chess-Shops.com	www.chess-shops.com
Cloud Top	www.cloudtop.co.uk
Colborne Trophies Limited	www.colbornetrophies. freeserve.co.uk
Crafts Unlimited	www.crafts-unlimited.co.uk/
Creations Direct	www.creationsdirect.co.uk
Cycle Centre Online	www.cyclestore.co.uk
D&R Supplies	www.tool-signshop.co.uk
Dales Cycles	www.dalescycles.com
Dirtbikestore	www.dirtbikestore.com
Discount Sports	www.discountsports.co.uk
DP Software	www.dpsoftware.co.uk
Ecycles	www.ecycles.uk.com
Finefettle	www.finefettle.com
Footlaunched	www.footlaunched.com

For a complete and current list of Which? Web Traders go to
www.which.net/webtrader

Fotosouvenirs	www.fotosouvenirs.com
Fusion Records	www.fusionrecords.co.uk
GENfair	www.genfair.com
Golf Mega Deals	www.golfmegadeals.com
Golf Shopper	www.golfshopper.co.uk
Heart Rate Monitor	www.heartratemonitor.co.uk/
Hip Action	www.hipaction.com
Hobbicraft	www.hobbicraft.co.uk
Jacksons Fishing Tackle	www.jackfish.net/
Joe Browns	www.joebrowns.co.uk
kinetics.org.uk	www.kinetics.org.uk
Klikit UK	www.klikit.co.uk
Ladyshield	www.ladyshield-stitchcrafts.co.uk
Laines world	www.lainesworld.co.uk
Live4outdoors	www.live4outdoors.com
National Sports Medicine Institute of the UK	www.nsmi.org.uk
Novelty Togs	www.noveltytogs.com
Oldham Trading	www.oldhamtrading.co.uk/
Ongolf.co.uk	www.ongolf.co.uk
Online Hobbies.co.uk	www.online-hobbies.co.uk/
Pier Models	www.PierModels.com
POP Enterprises	www.p-o-p.demon.co.uk
Prendas Ciclismo	www.prendas.co.uk
Proops Brothers	www.proopsbrothers.com

SPORTS & HOBBIES

For a complete and current list of Which? Web Traders go to
www.which.net/webtrader

Punctilio Modelspot	www.modelspot.com
Purple Beaver	www.purplebeaver.net
Qvpennies	www.qvpennies.com
Rock + Run (Climb Ltd)	www.rockrun.com
Rockfax	www.rockfax.com
Saddle Sore	www.saddlesore.co.uk
Shop!	www.shop-tv.co.uk
Singletrack Bikes	www.singletrack.co.uk
Skate Pool	www.skatepool.com
Skydragons	www.skydragons.com
Sport Shop Online	www.sportshoponline.co.uk
Sportsbras	www.sportsbras.co.uk
Sportsmart	www.sportsmart.co.uk
Sportswearhouse	www.sportswearhouse.co.uk
sportyshop	www.sportyshop.co.uk/
Stadium Intersports	www.stadium-intersport.com
Stitchworld	www.stitchworld.co.uk
Tack Up	www.tackandski.co.uk
Tackleshop	www.tackleshop.co.uk
Tax Free Golf	www.taxfreegolf.com/
tennisnuts	www.tennisnuts.com/
Terminator	www.terminator.co.uk
The Pro Shop	www.theproshop.co.uk
The Sport Archive	www.thesportarchive.com
The Watershed	www.the-watershed.co.uk

SPORTS & HOBBIES

For a complete and current list of Which? Web Traders go to
www.which.net/webtrader

Trailbuzz	www.trailbuzz.com/
Trout Fishing Online	www.troutfishing.co.uk
Up and Under	www.upandunder.co.uk

Toys, babies and kids

Activity Toys	www.activekid.co.uk
Adventure Shop	www.adventureshop.co.uk
Alpha Toymaster	www.alphatoymaster.co.uk/
Babycare Direct	www.babycare-direct.co.uk/
Babymilk Action	www.babymilkaction.org/
Babyworld	www.babyworld.com
Buckie Bears	www.buckiebears.mcmail.com/
Charlie Crow Costumes	www.charliecrow.com/
Company of Bears	www.companyofbears.com
Dawson & Son	www.dawson-and-son.com
eToys	www.etoys.co.uk
Fun and Games	www.funandgamestoyshop.co.uk
Grannie Annie's	www.grannie-annie.co.uk
Grobag	www.grobag.co.uk/
Honfleur Christening Gowns	www.honfleur.co.uk
Hugs and Cuddles	www.hugsandcuddles.co.uk
Little by Little	www.littlebylittle.co.uk/ system/index.html
Little Wonders	www.littlewonders.co.uk
Mums2000	www.mums2000.com/

For a complete and current list of Which? Web Traders go to
www.which.net/webtrader

TOYS, BABIES & KIDS

Over The Moon Babywear	www.overthemoon-babywear.co.uk
Pet Pen Pals	www.petpenpals.co.uk
Planetbaby	www.planetbaby.co.uk
Playbug	www.playbug.com/
Popcorn Live	www.popcornlive.co.uk
Senatoys	www.senatoys.co.uk
Shop!	www.shop-tv.co.uk
Strongcrafts	www.malltraders.com/strongcrafts
Teddy Bear UK	www.teddy-bear-uk.com
Teeny-tots.com	www.teeny-tots.com/
Thetoyshop.com	www.thetoyshop.com
Toy centre	www.toycentre.com
Toybugs	www.toybugs.com
Twinkle Twinkle	www.twinkleontheweb.co.uk/
Urchin	www.urchin.co.uk
WoodenToy Store	www.woodentoystore.co.uk/

TOYS, BABIES & KIDS

For a complete and current list of Which? Web Traders go to
www.which.net/webtrader

Travel

ABC Holiday Extras	www.holidayextras.co.uk
B&B NET	www.ukbnb.net
Bargain Holidays	www.bargainholidays.com
B-Driven	www.b-driven.com/
Caledonia Homes	www.florida-villas.com
CO-OP Travelcare	www.coop.co.uk/
Eurodestination	www.eurodestination.com
Eurotours	www.eurotours.co.uk
Flipflops	www.flipflops.co.uk
flynow.com	www.flynow.com
Global Travel	www.globalholidays.co.uk
Go Fly Limited	www.go-fly.com
Going Places	www.goplaces.co.uk
Grip Maps	www.gripmaps.com/
Holiday Autos	www.holidayautos.co.uk
Hudson Leathershop	www.hudsonleathershop.co.uk
Hugh Lewis	www.outdoor-leisure.com
Instant Holidays	www.instant-holidays.com
lastminute.com	www.lastminute.com
Leisure Hunt	www.leisurehunt.com
Maps Worldwide	www.mapsworldwide.co.uk
Navigator Travel	www.navigatortravel.co.uk/
Norwich Union Direct	www.norwich-union.co.uk/

T R A V E L

For a complete and current list of Which? Web Traders go to
www.which.net/webtrader

The Which? Guide to Shopping on the Internet

Options Insurance	www.optionsinsurance.co.uk/
Outdoor Mega Store	www.outdoormegastore.co.uk/
Safariquip	www.safariquip.co.uk/
Shetland Wildlife Tours	www.shetland-wildlife-tours.zetnet.co.uk
Skiers Travel Bureau	www.skiers-travel.co.uk
Snowline	www.snow-line.co.uk
Spotlight Guides Ltd	www.coast2coast.co.uk
Travel Care	www.travelcareonline.com
Travel Plan Direct	www.travelplan-direct.co.uk/
Travel Store	www.travelstore.com
Travelwise	www.travelwise-uk.com
UK Chauffeurs	www.uk-chauffeurs.com
Worldwide Travel Insurance Services	www.wwtis.co.uk

For a complete and current list of Which? Web Traders go to
www.which.net/webtrader

Part 4

Information sites

Information sites

It can often be useful to be armed with background information on the type of product you want before you shop. This applies to high-street shops as well as web sites. The list below highlights some of the specialist information sites that can help you in choosing your purchase. Some of the sites listed also sell products but their principal function is to provide information. For example, it is worth looking at publishers' web sites to find out what new books are available and to read interviews with authors.

Remember, too, that many of the shopping sites listed in the Web Directory in Part 2 with 'buying guide' and advice features or product-comparison tables have genuinely useful information on products and what to look for.

Depending on what type of product you want, you could also look at the product reviews in online versions of established magazines such as *What HiFi* or *AutoExpress*. *Which?* provides useful independent buying information on a wide range of products and publishes all its product testing reports on Which? Online (**www.which.net**). You have to be a Which? Member to see them – details are on the site. Alternatively, visit your local library to see the latest *Which?* reports for free and use the buying information to help you surf for the best deal when you get home.

Art and antiques

Antiquesworld.co.uk

One of the best general antiques sites. All the latest news on antiques and collectables, including details of fairs and events. Lots of links to other useful related sites.

Art-review.co.uk

Keep up with contemporary art. Modern art news, reviews, profiles of young, up-and-coming artists plus listings of exhibitions and shows all over the UK.

Books and magazines

Bibliofind.com

US-based second-hand/rare book site owned by Amazon. You can't buy from this site but its huge database of booksellers lets you search for the title you want. Type in the title or author and Bibliofind comes up with cost, book condition and contact details for the shops or dealers you can buy from.

WORTH A LOOK: 'Collectors' Guides' section includes information on buying rare books, including guidance on how to identify a first edition

DELIVERY: set by individual booksellers

Books.guardian.co.uk

Read reviews on the latest book releases, including children's books. Plus read first chapters of selected books, see the bestseller lists, find out about authors or join a chat forum. An excellent site from the *Guardian*.

Bookwire.com

Inside information on the book business. US bias but worth looking at for author interviews, features, reviews and links to book-related sites.

Penguin.co.uk

Includes a book of the day and author of the day, a special guest author each month, details of what new books have been published that month. Also Penguin Readers Group, audio books and children's titles.

---

theBookseller.com

Web site of the weekly trade newspaper, *The Bookseller*. Includes interviews with authors, bestseller charts, publishing news and job adverts.

Cars

Autoexpress.co.uk

A mass of useful information to help you buy. Latest car reviews plus crash tests, product tests and general car news and features. You need to register first to get most of the info.

Carprices.co.uk

Before you buy a used car, check out the regularly updated used-car pricing details on this site. Over 150,000 prices listed.

Whatcar.co.uk

Over 1,000 road tests online. New car search facility to help you find the car you want. Tests on products such as child car seats. Lots of general buying advice.

Children

Parentsoup.com

Popular US site but still relevant to UK parents. Almost everything you could ever want to know about bringing up children, including general product buying advice. Chat forums useful for finding out views of other parents.

Webbaby.co.uk

As well as a wealth of general information for new and soon-to-be parents, this site has a 'Baby Gear Guide' with buying guide articles on products such as car seats, buggies, cots and toddlers' bikes.

Clothes and fashion

Fashionbot.com

Key in the type of clothing you are after – for example, fleeces, jackets or more specifically, a red shirt for a woman – and this search engine will come up with a range from the Arcadia Group of shops. These include Top Shop, Principles, Racing Green, Burton and Dorothy Perkins.

Handbag.com

See the latest styles and read fashion features at this online women's magazine. Lots of make-up and beauty product advice too.

Vogue.co.uk

Fashion news and views. Previews of next season's looks plus the current season's hottest trends. 'Street Chic' section for street-style ideas and interviews with designers.

Computers and electrical goods

Ecoustics.com

Online audio and video magazine. US-based but with useful equipment buying guides plus lists of links to other specialist sites and online magazines.

Gamespy.com

US site with gaming gossip, news, reviews and features for the serious computer games player.

Itreviews.co.uk

Site jam-packed with independent reviews of myriad computer-related products plus digital cameras, DVD and MP3 players. 'Group test' articles point out pros and cons of a range of similar products. Forum for exchanging views on products.

Pricewatch.co.uk

Price-comparison site specialising in making comparisons for computer hardware and software. The computer sites searched are clearly listed. Also makes comparisons for a few other products including DVDs and videos.

Whathifi.com

Site of leading hifi and home cinema magazine. Helpful buying guides on hifi, video and DVD equipment plus potentially useful chat room.

Zdnet.co.uk

Technology magazine site with emphasis on computers and software. Product reviews on everything from printers to computer notebooks. Geared more towards the computer buff than the complete beginner.

DIY/home improvement

Designstudio.com

World of Interiors magazine's online directory of fabric and wallpaper designs. Browse through hundreds of samples, make up a swatchboard and find a local stockist.

Diyfixit.co.uk

Step-by-step guides to a huge range of DIY jobs around the home with details of how to choose the products you need.

Fmb.org.uk/consumers

Consumer section of the Federation of Master Builders web site. Useful for details on the FMB Code of Practice, advice on how to steer clear of cowboy builders, dealing with household emergencies plus a range of other builder-orientated articles.

Improveline.com

Site to help you find home-improvement contractors or tradespeople, whether it's for a leaky tap or to build an extension to your home. Covers aspects such as customer references, insurance and previous projects for each tradesperson registered with the site. Also has general advice on dealing with contractors, details on regulations and decorating ideas.

Theplumber.com

US site devoted to plumbing, aimed at DIYers as well as professionals. Discussion forums, plumbing advice and articles – and, for the deeply interested plumbing buff, a brief history of plumbing.

Financial services

Annuity-bureau.co.uk

This is a useful information site for different types of pension.

Apcims.co.uk

Home of the Association of Private Client Investment Managers and Stockbrokers. Guide to brokers and their services.

Bankfacts.org.uk

Home of the British Bankers' Association. Information about use of bank accounts, payment methods etc. including guidance on shopping online.

Eiris.org

Site of the Ethical Investment Research Service. Guidance on choosing investment funds which invest ethically.

Find.co.uk

The site to visit if you want an extensive directory of financial web sites. Instant access to over 5,000 financial web site links. The site is split into various sections – for example, Mortgages and Loans, Banking and Savings and Information Services.

Fsa.gov.uk

Site of Financial Services Authority, the regulatory body for the financial services industry. Your rights plus general advice on buying financial products. The FSA can check to make sure the financial institution you want to deal with is legitimate.

Ft.com

Definitive site for business and financial news and stock market, company and fund data analysis.

Hemscott.co.uk

Company information specialist – share prices, charts, background information etc

Micropal.com

Comprehensive analysis and listing of investment funds.

Moneyextra.com

Useful comparison site which helps you compare deals on mortgages, travel and life insurance, bank accounts, loans and ISAs. Take a look at the Moneyextra club – an investment-focused club you can use to exchange investment ideas online, get stockmarket email alerts plus discounts on a range of products and services.

Moneyfacts.co.uk

Web site of the publisher of *Moneyfacts,* a trade financial monthly, and of *Life Pensions* and *Business Moneyfacts.* Useful financial information.

Moneynet.co.uk

Lots of independent advice and information. Clear data comparing different mortgages, personal loans, credit cards and savings accounts. A remortgage calculator helps you find out how much you can save by moving your mortgage and who offers the best deal.

Proshare.org.uk

Information about direct investment in shares including investment clubs.

Food

Cheese.com

Curious but strangely fascinating site devoted entirely to cheese. Read the latest cheese news or, more usefully perhaps, search Cheese.com's extensive database for details on different types of cheeses from all over the world.

Organicfood.co.uk

Organic food and lifestyle information web site. Includes large database of organic retailers, reviews of home-delivery services, chat zone and articles on issues such as GM foods, and animal health and welfare.

Simplyfood.co.uk

Food and wine site from Carlton TV. Gadget reviews on products such as breadmakers and corkscrews, cookery book reviews and taste-test results plus recipe features, wine-buying guides and food news.

Garden

Expertgardener.com

Useful news and gardening community site. Exchange views in a range of forums, including the 'urban garden community' and the 'ecological garden community'.

Gardenweb.com

Discussion forums for gardeners. Exchange views on garden problems and products. Site also has plant dictionary, glossary of botanical terms and garden bookstore.

Gardenworld.co.uk

Comprehensive site with listings of local garden centres, product and plant suppliers. Details on new gardening products (e.g. the SMART laser lawnmower), gardening events listings and links to many other gardening sites.

Nhm.ac.uk

A postcode plant database from the Natural History Museum. Look up which plants are native to your area (and therefore which will grow best and benefit surrounding wildlife). Site includes lists of suppliers of British-origin seeds and plants.

Health

Homeopathyhome.com

Directory of homeopathic organisations, reference library with articles and details of recent research, details of where to get homeopathic products plus lots of general info for those new to homeopathy.

Nhsdirect.nhs.uk

Official NHS patients' site. Features include guide to treating common symptoms at home, over 200 audio clips on a wide range of health topics and links to thousands of sources of help and advice.

Surgerydoor.co.uk

Extensive magazine-style health information site fronted by TV GP, Dr Mark Porter. Covers many topics from what to keep in the medicine cabinet to information on surgical operations. Sections on complementary medicine, NHS and travel health.

Music and film

Classicalmusic.co.uk

Features, reviews, guides and concert listings. Video interviews with classical artists and live classical web casts. Links to many other sites of interest to classical fans.

Dotmusic.co.uk

Site boasting latest news and reviews of rock, pop and dance sounds. 'Release schedule' section keeps you up-to-date with forthcoming releases so you can get your order in quick.

film.guardian.co.uk

Another information site from the *Guardian*. Video section has reviews of rental, retail and DVD current releases, and releases going back a few months. *Guardian* and *Observer* 'choice' section for recommended titles.

Imdb.com

Owned by Amazon, The Internet Movie Database is packed with all the latest details on new releases, plus search for plot outlines and reviews of almost any film you may think of buying or renting. Lots of US film information so you know what will be showing here soon.

Sports

Bikemagic.com

News and bike and gadget reviews for the serious cycling fan. Classified ads section plus links to other cycling sites.

Fishing.co.uk

Informative site covering all types of fishing. Use the 'Locator' to find tackle shops and fisheries. Articles to help you choose the best tackle. 'Clubroom' for chat plus calendar of events.

Golftoday.co.uk

Golf magazine site with all the information you could ever need on the sport. Links to other sites, discussion forums and articles on new products.

Ifyouski.com

Ski web site offering snow and weather reports, information on insurance, resorts, gear and holidays, and ski championships.

Runnersworld.com

Serious-looking US site useful for UK runners too. Detailed section on shoes and running gear with shoe reviews, general buying guides and information on accessories such as sports watches.

Ski.co.uk

Basic-looking site but useful for its directory of shops and sites selling ski clothing and equipment.

Sporting-life.com

Popular multi-sports web site based in Leeds. General news and results, events and match listings, betting news and fanzine-style information on a wide range of popular sports.

Travel

Tips4trips.com

Handy site full of well-meaning tips provided by other travellers to help keep your holiday stress-free. Section on 'What to Pack' is full of ideas for products and gadgets to take with you.

Travel.world.co.uk

Large index of European travel agents and tour operators. Click on the type of holiday you want – for example boating/sailing holidays or city breaks – and you are presented with a list of travel companies you can link to. Also information on airlines, hotel chains, self-catering and car hire.

Wine and beer

Decanter.com

Wine news and information from *Decanter* magazine. 'Wine finder' search facility, useful wine tasting and buying information for beginners plus lots of features for connoisseurs.

Wine-pages.com

Informative, unflashy site run by Tom Cannavan, a wine journalist. Lots of tasting results on 'value' as well as expensive wines. Site users are invited to send in their own tasting notes for publication. Weekly round-up of tips from UK's leading newspaper wine columnists.

Beer

Beerhunter.com

Web site of Michael Jackson. A writer, broadcaster and connoisseur of beer. His tireless quest to seek out the finest beers from around the world has earned him the title 'the Beer Hunter'.

Beersite.com

A search engine dedicated to everything beer- and brewing-related. Most of the links are to US web sites

Breworld.com

Features, news, articles, competitions and plenty of useful links.

Camra.org.uk

Web site of the Campaign for Real Ale. Many of its regional branches have their own web sites.

Protzonbeer.com

Web site of Roger Protz, editor of *The Good Beer Guide* (published by CAMRA). Writer and broadcaster, described by *Time Out* as 'the King of Beer Writers.'

Appendix

Setting yourself up with the Internet

Setting yourself up with the Internet

It is all too easy to get turned off using the Internet by the glitches and technical difficulties that can often occur. This is where making sure you have a good ISP (Internet Service Provider) and decent, relatively up-to-date equipment can significantly enhance your Internet and your online shopping experiences.

Your equipment

If your PC can work with Windows 95 or a later version, or your Apple Macintosh with System 7 or a later version, it will be able to use most or all of the latest Internet software. If you are planning to buy a new PC or Apple Mac, make sure you have the latest Windows or System software pre-installed. Check the processor runs at 133MHz or faster and that you have at least 32Mb of main memory. It makes sense to buy a large-capacity hard drive as software increasingly requires more space. Make sure your monitor/graphics adaptor can display images at a resolution of at least 800 times 600. You'll need a sound card and speakers too if you want the full multi-media Internet experience.

Choosing a modem

Most people who use the Internet at home currently link up to it via a modem (modulator-demodulator). This is a unit that converts computer information into 'rasps and squeals' that can be sent over a telephone line to another computer. Many new computers are sold with a modem already built-in. Otherwise, you need to buy an external modem which sits outside the computer at the end of a special cable. (You can buy internal modems you can fit yourself, but this is only worth attempting if you are an expert.)

The speed of your modem is all-important. It is this that determines how quickly information can move between your computer and the Internet. A slow modem is fine if you are planning to use the Internet only once in a while, but it can make your Internet experience very frustrating, especially if you want to browse a few shopping sites. If you are likely to use the Internet on a fairly regular basis then go for a faster modem. The speed at which a modem can transfer information is described in bits per second (bps) or thousands of bits per second (kbps). Modem speeds are constantly being developed and improved. It is worth buying the fastest modem you can – 56 kbps is the current standard.

Faster ways to link up

Heavy Internet users may find the alternatives to a modem more convenient because they offer a faster connection. ISDN (Integrated Services Digital Network) is a digital-only connection to the existing telephone system. An ISDN link creates a connection to the Internet within a second or so compared with as much as 45 seconds for a conventional modem. You pay for what you get, however, and ISDN is worthwhile only if you use the Internet heavily. A better option for home-users wanting a speedier connection is BT's Home Highway. This is a simplified version of ISDN that is cheaper to install and still faster than a modem. If you opt for this, your old phone line will be converted into two digital lines which will enable the faster links to take place.

A more recent and faster option than ISDN is called

ADSL (Asymmetric Digital Subscriber Line). This also offers a permanent link to the Internet so that, for example, web pages appear more quickly and email is received almost instantly. This can offer better value than ISDN for the home-user although it is not yet available in all areas of the UK.

Cable modem access to the Internet is also available and offers similar features to ADSL for a similar cost. Like ADSL, the service is not yet available nationwide. Both ISDN and ADSL use a terminal adapter and/or a network card in the PC, not a conventional modem.

High-speed Internet access is also available by satellite. This is very fast but the cost for the average home-user (just over £1,000 for the hardware, plus extra depending on the amount of information you receive over the Internet) means it is not currently an attractive option.

For most home-users, connection to the Internet via a modem is still the most realistic option. This is partly because of the cost but also because only a minority of ISPs are able to accept the more sophisticated connections.

Choosing an ISP

An Internet Service Provider acts as the middleman connecting your modem to a much larger, more powerful computer that forms part of the Internet. Some ISPs charge for their service while others provide it for free. At one extreme, some of the ISPs that charge do so by making you pay for both Internet access and call charges by the minute so that the more you access and use the Internet, the more you pay. At the other end of the spectrum, some ISPs provide free access and calls, although some kind of 'up-front' payment may be necessary. (For example, BT SurfTogether and Freeserve Anytime offer free calls for a set monthly fee.) In the middle are schemes that variously require a fixed monthly payment on top of call charges or just charge for calls or provide free calls at certain times of the day or week.

It may seem odd to consider paying for an ISP's service when you can get it for free, but there are a number of things to consider before you sign up. The most important is to find out what kind of service the ISP provides.

ISPs provide software which lets you use Internet facilities but some ISPs skimp on the software they provide which may mean you are denied access to some Internet facilities such as more advanced forms of email. Check if you are being offered anything more than a 'web browser'. If not, you are unlikely to be getting the best from your connection.

Free services often make their money by charging for technical support. If you think you might need lots of help when you are setting up, they may not be your best option. These ISPs can also be very busy at weekends and in the evenings, making it harder to get online and they often carry lots of advertising.

Some ISPs just offer basic access to the Internet whilst others offer more. ISPs that charge a monthly fee may provide a range of 'channels' covering areas such as shopping, news, finance and health. They may also offer established discussion groups and chat rooms. This can be helpful if you prefer to have a firm starting point for using the Internet. It means you do not have to put so much effort into searching for things on the Net because the ISP provides lots of information and simple links to a range of potentially useful sites in order to make the whole process easier for you. On the negative side, this can limit the Internet experience for less adventurous users because they do not have to explore it.

Some subscription services, such as AOL, provide special software designed to enhance your Internet experience – for example, software with features that enable parents to define the type of content their children can view. The main disadvantage of subscription services is the cost, although individual ISPs may charge different rates depending on how much and when you use the service.

When you are choosing your ISP, think about the kind of service you want and how much you are willing to pay. Just as with other goods and services, it pays to shop around for the deal that suits you best. You should aim to try before you sign up. Many ISPs offer a free trial – take them up on it and see what you think (although remember to cancel if you are not impressed as you will have had to give your credit card details).

For more detailed information on computers and the Internet, see the following Which? titles:
The Which? Guide to Computers, The Which? Guide to the Internet and *The Which? Computer Troubleshooter.*

Index

WEB SITE REPORT FORM

We would be interested to read about your experiences of shopping on the Internet and of any web sites you wish to recommend. Please fill in the following report form and send to Department VF, FREEPOST, Which? Books, 2 Marylebone Road, London NW1 4DF (you don't need a stamp). You can also email your report to internetshopping@which.net

---

Personal details

Name:

Address:

Telephone number:

Email:

Which? Membership number (if relevant):

Web site report

Address of site (URL):   Is it UK based?

What were you trying to buy?

Did you succeed in buying it?

How easy was it to place your order?:
☐ Very   ☐ Fairly   ☐ Not very   ☐ Difficult

Did you receive confirmation of your order?   ☐ Yes   ☐ No

What delivery time was stipulated on the web site?

How many days did it actually take for the item to be delivered?

Means of delivery?   ☐ Post   ☐ Courier   ☐ Other

Did you have to return the item?   ☐ Yes   ☐ No
(because it was not what you wanted/was broken/was the wrong colour/did not match the description)

Any other comments about this site? _____

_____

_____

SATISFACTION GRID

Design of site

☑ Very satisfied ☐ Fairly satisfied ☐ Not very ☐ Not at all

Ease of ordering

☐ Very satisfied ☐ Fairly satisfied ☐ Not very ☐ Not at all

Speed of delivery

☐ Very satisfied ☐ Fairly satisfied ☐ Not very ☐ Not at all

Would you buy from the site again? ☐ Yes ☐ No

Would you buy anything over the Internet again? ☐ Yes ☐ No

Readers' recommendations

Please let us know of any web sites that you have found particularly easy
to use or with outstanding good service.

WHICH? BOOKS

The following titles were available as this book went to press.

General reference (legal, financial, practical, etc.)
Be Your Own Financial Adviser
420 Legal Problems Solved
150 Letters that Get Results
What to Do When Someone Dies
The Which? Computer Troubleshooter
The Which? Guide to an Active Retirement
The Which? Guide to Changing Careers
The Which? Guide to Choosing a Career
The Which? Guide to Computers
The Which? Guide to Computers for Small Businesses
The Which? Guide to Divorce
The Which? Guide to Doing Your Own Conveyancing
The Which? Guide to Domestic Help
The Which? Guide to Employment
The Which? Guide to Gambling
The Which? Guide to Getting Married
The Which? Guide to Giving and Inheriting
The Which? Guide to Going Digital
The Which? Guide to Home Safety and Security
The Which? Guide to Insurance
The Which? Guide to the Internet
The Which? Guide to Money
The Which? Guide to Pensions
The Which? Guide to Renting and Letting
The Which? Guide to Shares
The Which? Guide to Starting Your Own Business
The Which? Guide to Working from Home
Which? Way to Buy, Own and Sell a Flat
Which? Way to Buy, Sell and Move House
Which? Way to Clean It
Which? Way to Drive Your Small Business
Which? Way to Manage Your Time -- and Your Life
Which? Way to Save and Invest
Which? Way to Save Tax
Wills and Probate

Action Pack (A5 wallet with forms and 28-page book inside)
Make Your Own Will

Health
Understanding HRT and the Menopause
The Which? Guide to Complementary Medicine

The Which? Guide to Children's Health
The Which? Guide to Managing Asthma
The Which? Guide to Managing Back Trouble
The Which? Guide to Managing Stress
The Which? Guide to Men's Health
The Which? Guide to Women's Health
Which? Medicine

Gardening
The Gardening Which? Guide to Growing Your Own Vegetables
The Gardening Which? Guide to Patio and Container Plants
The Gardening Which? Guide to Small Gardens
The Gardening Which? Guide to Successful Perennials
The Gardening Which? Guide to Successful Propagation
The Gardening Which? Guide to Successful Pruning
The Gardening Which? Guide to Successful Shrubs

Do-it-yourself
The Which? Book of Do-It-Yourself
The Which? Book of Plumbing and Central Heating
The Which? Book of Wiring and Lighting
Which? Way to Fix It

Travel/leisure
The Good Bed and Breakfast Guide
The Good Food Guide
The Good Skiing and Snowboarding Guide
The Good Walks Guide
The Which? Guide to Country Pubs
The Which? Guide to Pub Walks
The Which? Guide to Scotland
The Which? Guide to Tourist Attractions
The Which? Guide to Weekend Breaks in Britain
The Which? Hotel Guide
The Which? Wine Guide
Which? Holiday Destination

Ringbinder with looseleaf pages and plastic wallet
Great Days Out

Available from bookshops, and by post from:
Which?, Dept TAZM, Castlemead,
Gascoyne Way, Hertford X, SG14 1LH
or phone FREE on (0800) 252100
quoting Dept TAZM and your credit card details